SPIRITUAL
DIRECTION

~ ~

SPIRITUAL DIRECTION

Principles and Practices

Robert F. Morneau

CROSSROAD · NEW YORK

1992

The Crossroad Publishing Company
370 Lexington Avenue, New York, NY 10017

Copyright © 1992 by Robert F. Morneau

Printed in the United States of America

Library of Congress Cataloging-in-Publication Data

Morneau, Robert F., 1938–
     Spiritual direction : principles and practices / Robert F. Morneau.
          p.   cm.
     Includes bibliographical references and index.
     ISBN 0-8245-1202-2 (pbk.)
     1. Spiritual direction. 2. Spiritual life—Catholic Church.
3. Catholic Church—Membership. I. Title
BX2350.7.M67 1992
253.5'3—dc20
                                                              92-18749
                                                                  CIP

Contents

PREFACE

When the prophet Elijah went into the wilderness (1 Kings 19:4–8), the Lord sent an angel to the prophet with this message: "Get up and eat, or the journey will be too long for you."

I have often found life's journey to be long; I have often been desirous of nourishment; I have often felt the need to be awakened by the Lord's messengers. One way of coping (and even, at times, thriving) on the journey has been to read the writings of people who reflectively offer their experiences and the lessons they have learned from life. With these companions — such as Romano Guardini, Alan Paton, William Shakespeare, John of the Cross, Catherine of Siena, Wallace Stegner, Teresa of Avila, Peter Berger, Dag Hammarskjold, Hermann Hesse, Michael Polanyi, Paul Tillich, Karl Rahner, James Joyce, Chaim Potok — the years have been enriched, indeed ennobled.

Over the pass twenty years or more I have been taking voluminous notes from these writers and others and every so often patterns emerged that indicate parallel thinking, sometimes even parallel lives. In various periodicals I have published these diverse gatherings, all dealing, in one way or another, with our spiritual journey. My hope is that the reader will find them as markings or intersections of grace and not distractions.

I express gratitude to the editors of the various magazines who have kindly let me reproduce these articles in their present, and somewhat edited, form.

ACKNOWLEDGMENTS

The chapters of this book first appeared as follows:

Chapter 1, "Principles of Prayer," in *Review for Religious* (May 1979); reprinted in *Discovering God's Presence* under the chapter title "Presence and Principles," 67–82

Chapter 2, "Principles of Discernment," in *Review for Religious* 41, no. 2 (March–April 1982): 161–75

Chapter 3, "Principles of Asceticism," in *Review for Religious* 44, no. 3 (May–June 1985): 410–25

Chapter 4, "Principles of Spiritual Direction," in *Chicago Studies* 26, no. 2 (August 1987): 122–38

Chapter 5, "Reverence," in *Emmanuel* 91, no. 1 (January–February 1985): 30–35

Chapter 6, "Spiritual Exercises for Eclectic Nomads," in *Pastoral Life* 30, no. 8 (September 1981): 9–16

Chapter 7, "Gaudeamus Igitur: In Defense of Joy," in *Pastoral Life* 31, no. 4 (April 1982): 2–8

Chapter 8, "Quaker Spirituality: Concepts and Concerns," in *Emmanuel* 92, no. 2 (March 1986): 74–81, and 93, no. 3 (April 1986), 132–37

PART ONE

Principles of Spirituality

Chapter 1

PRINCIPLES OF PRAYER

To grow in our relationship with one another or with God demands an ongoing process of communication. Prayer is necessary for growth in our relationship with God since it establishes a dialogue that allows a mutual exchange between God's concerns and our needs and gifts. In order that prayer might be meaningful, certain principles must be known and experienced because they outline universal conditions that are necessary for meaningful communication.

This chapter culls out ten principles from a variety of sources. Different spiritual authors, experiencing prayer from the perspective of their unique personalities, share in written form what has been helpful to them as they attempt to dialogue with God. Their articulated experiences can be helpful to us as we examine and evaluate our own attempts to deepen our relationship with the living and true God.

A three-step method will be used: (1) a statement of a principle of prayer; (2) a series of quotations that gives the source of the principle or demonstrates its effects; and (3) a commentary developing various implications buried within the principle and/or quotations.

Though principles are significant in and of themselves and can be advantageous in providing a sense of direction, experience itself is the central concern. Hopefully, as we journey beyond the principle into the lived experience that it elucidates, we will find deeper meaning and come into more intimate contact with the principal Reality underlying all principles.

1. Prayer is essentially loving attention.[1]

Thus the individual also should proceed only with a loving attention to God, without making specific acts. He should conduct himself passively, as we have said, without efforts of his own, but with the simple, loving awareness, as a person who opens his eyes with loving attention.[2]

~

Attention animated by desire is the whole foundation of religious practices.[3]

~

I shall not dwell upon this because I want to say something about the way in which I think those of us who practice prayer may profit though everything is profitable to a soul that loves the Lord with fervent desire, since it instills into it courage and wonder.[4]

Two essential elements of authentic prayer are contained in the definition of prayer as loving attention: awareness of the presence of the Other and a heartfelt, concerned response. Distractions within consciousness and indifference of the heart block meaningful communication with God. If, on our part, we are called to love with attention, this is always consequent upon God's loving attention directed toward us. God our creator not only made us but is attentive to the smallest detail of our lives. God's love is complete and faithful. When William Blake asked the large question, "Did he smile his work to see?," the answer is in the affirmative.

1. See John 17; Rom. 11: 33–36.

2. *The Collected Works of St. John of the Cross*, trans. Kieran Kavanaugh, O.C.D., and Otilio Rodriguez, O.C.D. (Washington, D.C.: ICS Publications, 1973), 622.

3. Simone Weil, *Waiting for God* (New York: Harper Colophon Books, 1951), 197.

4. *The Complete Works of St. Teresa of Jesus*, ed. and trans. E. Allison Peers (London: Sheed & Ward, 1944), 2:363.

God's loving attention has been revealed in a unique way in Jesus, the Word incarnate. This coming-to-visit verifies God's love and awareness. Further verification is found in the gift of the Holy Spirit, a Spirit of love and knowledge. Because of this uncreated grace we are empowered to pray:

> The Spirit too comes to help us in our weakness. For when we cannot choose words in order to pray properly, the Spirit himself expresses our plea in a way that could never be put into words, and God who knows everything in our hearts knows perfectly well what he means, and that the pleas of the saints expressed by the Spirit are according to the mind of God. (Rom. 8:26–27)

Defining prayer in terms of loving attention is simple but not simplistic. Its simplicity lies in its directness and succinctness; it is not reductionistic because neither love nor attentiveness is easily attained. And there is always the classic example of King Claudius, the murderous uncle of Hamlet. Without attention, without love, prayer goes nowhere:

> My words fly up, my thoughts remain below:
> Words without thoughts never to heaven go.[5]

2. Prayer is proportionate to the quality of one's love.[6]

> Farewell, farewell! but this I tell
> To thee, thou Wedding-Guest!
> He prayeth well, who loveth well
> Both man and bird and beast.
>
> He prayeth best, who loveth best
> All things both great and small;
> For the dear God who loveth us,
> He made and loveth all.[7]

~

---

5. Hamlet III, iii, 97–98.
6. See 1 John 2:9–11; Luke 4:42–44.
7. Samuel Taylor Coleridge, "The Rime of the Ancient Mariner."

[St. Francis] knew that without prayer true love was impossible and that without love prayer became self-centered and barren.[8]

~

I repeat that if you have this in view you must not build upon foundations of prayer and contemplation alone, for, unless you strive after the virtues and practice them, you will never grow to be more than dwarfs. God grant that nothing worse than this may happen — for, as you know, anyone who fails to go forward begins to go back, and love, I believe, can never be content to say for long where it is.[9]

The spiritual life demands balance. How one relates to God in prayer is intimately connected to how one encounters his or her neighbor. Scripture is emphatic on this point: people who claim that they love God and simultaneously hate their neighbor are liars (John 2). On a lesser scale, anyone who spends hours in prayer while neglecting obvious needs of people close at hand must seriously examine the authenticity of such prayer. Indeed, the touchstone of genuine prayer is fraternal charity.[10]

Prayer and love are symbiotic. Since God is Love, we must go to the divine fount to receive this gift. Further, unless we share the love we receive from the gratuity of God, the divine gift begins to dry up or engender pride. As in all provinces of life, the principle of interdependence is operative here. The challenge is to integrate prayer and love, contemplation and virtue, liturgy and apostolate. Failure to do this leads to the privatization of religion and results in the great scandal of separating faith from everyday life. True imitation of Christ is manifest in an integrated spirituality that refuses to compartmentalize our relationship with God.

---

8. Murray Bodo, *Francis: The Journey and the Dream* (Cincinnati: St. Anthony Messenger Press, 1972), 64.

9. *The Complete Works of St. Teresa of Jesus*, 2:347.

10. *Spiritual Renewal of the American Priesthood* (Washington, D.C.: Publications Office, United States Catholic Conference, 1973), 48.

Evelyn Underhill succinctly captures this second principle: "To be unloving is to be out of touch with God."[11] Genuine prayer puts us in touch with God; real love bonds us with our brothers and sisters.

3. Genuine prayer demands some control over body and spirit.[12]

... we shall not fail to observe the fasts, disciplines and periods of silence which the order commands: for, as you know, if prayer is to be genuine it must be reinforced with these things — prayer cannot be accompanied by self-indulgence.[13]

~

Oh, who can tell how impossible it is for a man with appetites to judge the things of God as they are.[14]

~

We shall have overcome a considerable obstacle when prayer and penance condition each other, for their unity will be able to become the guarantee of their orientation. If it is necessary to deprive oneself of food and sleep, it is not to establish a performance or glorify oneself over an exploit, but to allow the spirit to give itself freely to prayer, since, if it is less strongly captivated by the things of earth, it will be able to give attention to what is above it.[15]

Addictions threaten the process of prayer. A body satiated with food, drinks, or drugs becomes listless and weary; a mind constantly filled with a flood of stimuli becomes unreceptive to other realities. Prayer is premised on the ability to say no at one level of existence in order to say yes to the workings of the Spirit.

---

11. *An Anthology of the Love of God from the Writings of Evelyn Underhill*, ed. Lumsden Barkway and Lucy Menzies (London: Mowbray & Co., 1976), 34.

12. See Gal. 5:16–23; Matt. 4:1–17.

13. *The Complete Works of St. Teresa of Jesus*, 2:16.

14. *The Collected Works of St. John of the Cross*, 364.

15. François Roustang, S.J., *Growth in the Spirit*, trans. Kathleen Pond (New York: Sheed & Ward, 1966), 232.

Asceticism is a condition that creates space and time for dialogue with God. Certain exercises, such as fasting, periods of extended silence, various forms of voluntary mortification, are means by which that space and time is made available for the visitations of our God. The "if–then" principle applies to our spirituality as it does to all human existence. If farmers desire an autumn harvest, then they must do the spring plowing and planting. If people want to listen and respond to God's will, then time and space must be given for that encounter to happen. Strong and determined desire lies at the root of such discipline.

Self-control extends one step beyond asceticism. Once the emptiness has been created through spiritual exercises done out of love, the soul must wait on the Lord. Waiting for God is at the heart of prayer and is already a deep form of prayer: self-control makes that waiting possible; grace makes it sacred. Although not speaking directly of prayer, C. S. Lewis describes well one aspect of our human condition: "Then came the worst part, the waiting."[16]

4. In prayer, I must bring this me to the living and true God.[17]

I enter into the presence of God with all my load of misery and troubles. And he takes me as I am and makes me to be alone with him.[18]

~

We pray with the door shut when without opening our mouths and in perfect silence we offer our petitions to the One who pays no attention to words but who looks hard at our hearts.[19]

~

16. C. S. Lewis, *The Last Battle* (New York: Collier Book, 1956), 13.

17. See Judg. 6:13; Rom. 7:14–25. This principle was presented in a guided retreat by Fr. William A. Peters, S.J.

18. *Raïssa's Journal*, presented by Jacques Maritain (Albany, N.Y.: Magi Books, 1963), 225.

19. *John Cassian: Conferences*, trans. and preface by Colm Luibheid with introduction by Owen Chadwick (New York: Paulist Press, 1985), 124.

I can testify that this is one of the most grievous kinds of life which I think can be imagined, for I had neither any joy in God nor any pleasure in the world. When I was in the midst of worldly pleasures, I was distressed by the remembrance of what I owed to God; when I was with God, I grew restless because of worldly affections.[20]

Any genuine conversation requires that each participant have a minimal level of self-knowledge and be familiar with the content under discussion. Where either is missing, communication breaks down. Prayer, a radical form of communication, requires the same: we must know our real self who addresses the living God and have some understanding of the experience being shared. Two major problems can lead to sterility in prayer. First, in desiring the approval of other, we, however unconsciously, hide or disguise our faults and sin thereby bringing a false self to prayer. Second, we falter in our conception of God. When this happens, the subject to whom we pray simply doesn't exist.

Psychologists describe a variety of selves that we should be aware of:

Each of us seems to have three *self-concepts*. The *personal* self-image is how the individual pictures his most inner self ("how I really am"). The *social* self is how he thinks others see him, and the pattern of responses he learns in order to be a social being. The *ideal* self is made up of the goals set by parents, the culture, and other sources ("how I should be"). Often, these three conflict, creating problems for the individual trying to satisfy them all.[21]

Each person must examine which of these selves is operative not only in the interactions of daily life but also in prayer. To play a role in the presence of the Lord prohibits encounter at the deepest level of our being. To demand perfection flowing

---

20. *The Complete Works of St. Teresa of Jesus*, 1:48.
21. John H. Brennecke and Robert G. Amick, *Psychology: Understanding Yourself* (Beverly Hills, Calif.: Benziger, Bruce & Glencoe, 1975), 43.

from the ideal self leads only to guilt. God invites us to come as we are, in our grace and sin.

Finite reason cannot comprehend the mystery of God. "My idea of God is not a divine idea. It has to be shattered time after time."[22] C. S. Lewis states this while holding that we can come to some knowledge of the living and true God. As Christians we come to this awareness through faith in Christ Jesus. In him, our God is made visible. Gifted with the Holy Spirit, we make our journey to the Father in and through Jesus. The paschal mystery is a summary statement of God's love and forgiveness. All prayer must pass through, and be enriched by, Jesus who speaks to the Father for us.

Authentic prayer demands authentic people. Our real self must be continually searched out; our real God sought in silence and solitude.

5. Prayer's primary focus is on God, not on self or on events.[23]

> I get nowhere by looking at myself: I merely get discouraged. So I am making the resolution to abandon myself entirely to God, look only at him, to leave all the care of myself to him, to practice only one thing, *confidence;* my extreme wretchedness, my nature cowardice, leaving me no other way to go to God and advance in good.[24]

~

> We knew too much of the knowable dark world,
> its secret and its sin,
> too little of God. And now we rise to see
> that even our pledges to humanity
> were false, since love must out of Love begin.[25]

~

---

22. C. S. Lewis, *A Grief Observed* (New York: Seabury Press, 1961), 52.

23. See Ps. 23; Gal. 2:17–21.

24. *Raïssa's Journal*, 83.

25. "Letter of Departure," *The Selected Poetry of Jessica Powers*, ed. Regina Seigfried and Robert Morneau (Kansas City: Sheed & Ward, 1989), 43–44.

The people of God are known in the world for the same things for which God is known. God's people should care about the same things that God cares for. Our purposes and priorities are the same. We love the same things, and hurt over the same things that God does.[26]

Two activities that are at the heart of our spirituality are focusing and centering. Through these activities we choose and/or discover what is at the core of our consciousness, a center that radically affects our thoughts, feelings and actions. Often a violent struggle rages in the deepest part of our being as various persons, forces, and things vie for centrality. A basic question for every pilgrim: what is the central focus of our life?

Prayer deals with centering. Personal experience gives evidence of how easily self-centeredness can dominate our lives and how daily anxieties can become so strong as to exclude any awareness of a loving, caring God. Self-transcendence is no easy task; trust that the Lord will provide for the smallest detail of our life demands deep faith. Only in grace can the obstacles blocking our encounter with God be removed. Jesus' prayer and life were centered on the Father and the doing of the divine will. Often in the early hours and before major events, Jesus explicitly turned to the Father in deep, familiar communication. These explicit moments were indications of an implicit, hidden life of union. How else can the intimacy of the Last Supper discourse be explained? Yet Jesus, embracing the fullness of humanity, must have struggled at times to keep proper focus. The agony in the garden points to that struggle whereby fear of suffering and any form of diminishment can distract us from one's mission.

The lives of the saints are records of people who struggled to make God the central focus of their lives. Augustine's ongoing conversion, Teresa of Avila's admission that for years her prayer was superficial, John of the Cross's constant challenge to mortification lest the self dominate — all manifest the con-

---

26. James Wallis, *The Call to Conversion* (San Francisco: Harper & Row, 1981), 143.

stant conflict between the ego and divine life. Marvelously God withholds rest from us that we might never be at peace until we center on the divine embrace. George Herbert (1593–1633), the great Anglican poet, perceived God as a pulley who offers us an authentic focus and center:

THE PULLEY

When God at first made man,
Having a glass of blessings standing by;
Let us (said he) pour on him all we can:
Let the world's riches, which dispersed lie,
    Contract into a span.

So strength first made a way;
Then beauty flow'd, then wisdom, honor, pleasure:
When almost all was out, God made a stay,
Perceiving that alone of all his treasure
    Rest in the bottom lay.

For if I should (said he)
Bestow this jewel also on my creature,
He would adore my gifts instead of me,
And rest in Nature, not the God of Nature:
    So both should losers be.

Yet let him keep the rest,
But keep them with repining restlessness:
Let him be rich and weary, that at least,
If goodness lead him not, yet weariness
    May toss him to my breast.[27]

6. Silence, solitude, and surrender are conditions for prayer.[28]

Twofold is the meaning of silence. One, the abstinence from speech, the absence of sound. Two, inner silence,

---

27. George Herbert, "The Pulley," *George Herbert: The Country Parson, The Temple*, ed. with an introduction by John N. Wall, Jr. (New York: Paulist Press, 1981), 284.

28. See Luke 22:39–46; Matt. 6:5–6.

the absence of self-concern, stillness. One may articulate words in his voice and yet be inwardly silent. One may abstain from uttering any sound and yet be overbearing.[29]

~

But I must not forget that, for me, being with people or even with one beloved person for any length of time without solitude is even worse. I lose my center. I feel dispersed, scattered, in pieces. I must have time alone in which to mull over any encounter, and to extract its juice, its essence, to understand what has really happened to me as a consequence of it.[30]

~

But what ultimately matters is not particular works, but a genuine, serious surrender of the person; the love which gives itself, that despises the calculated risk, and yet because it is so utterly in earnest, never for a moment overlooks the practical aspects.[31]

Silence, solitude, and surrender (the SSS principle) establishes the dispositions necessary for union with God. Simply by looking at their opposites we realize how significant and essential they are. Constant chatter precludes prayer ("In your prayers do not babble as the pagans do" — Matt. 6: 5); crowding our lives with activities and people does not leave room for the coming of God; clutching frantically to our own wills thwarts the realization of God's design.

In our acquisitive, noisy, and grasping culture, the dispositions of silence, solitude, and surrender are an endangered species. We must assess continuously the influence of the external environment upon our internal milieu. Diligence and discipline are required if we are to grow in a rich, interior silence; courage and trust empower us to venture into that

29. Abraham J. Heschel, *Man's Quest for God* (New York: Scribner's Sons, 1954), 44.

30. May Sarton, *Journal of a Solitude* (New York: W. W. Norton & Co., 1973), 195–96.

31. Hans Urs von Balthasar, *Prayer*, trans. A. V. Littledale (New York: Sheed & Ward, 1961), 182.

solitude where God awaits our presence; love and generosity release the deadly clasp we have on our fragile egos and permit us to make God the central reference point of our lives.

Attainment of a given end necessitates appropriate means. The house of the Lord has three gates before it: silence, solitude, and surrender. Only by passing through these narrow and, at times, treacherous openings can we hope to gain oneness with our God. Desire for union provides the energy to venture into these dispositions and the perseverance to stay with the task when things get difficult. There is ultimately only one tragedy (à la Leon Bloy): to retain a false ego and counterfeit freedom by failing, in silence, solitude, and surrender, to find the Lord.

7. *The tone of prayer is one of reverence, wonder, and awe.*[32]

Oh, how blessed is this soul who while still in her mortal body enjoys the reward of immortality! She holds all things in reverence, the left hand as well as the right, trouble as well as consolation, hunger and thirst as well as eating and drinking, cold and heat and nakedness as well as clothing, life as well as death, honor as well as disgrace, distress as well as comfort.[33]

~

Earth's crammed with heaven
And every common bush afire with God;
And only he who sees takes off his shoes —
The rest sit round and pluck blackberries.[34]

~

Thus, as children, you experienced two of the most important things men ever know — the wonder of life and the wonder of the universe, the wonder of life within the wonder of the universe. More important, you knew them

---

32. See Isa. 6:1–9; Ps. 118:5–7.

33. *Catherine of Siena: The Dialogue*, trans. and introduction by Suzanne Noffke, O.P. (New York: Paulist Press, 1980), 292.

34. Elizabeth Barrett Browning, "Aurora Leigh."

not from books, not from lectures, but simply from living among them. Most important, you knew them with reverence and awe — that reverence and awe that has died out of the modern world and been replaced by man's monkeylike amazement at the cleverness of his own inventive brain.[35]

A personal attitude toward a particular person or object is known as tone. Hostility, lack of openness, and prejudices are negative attitudes creating an atmosphere (tone) of fear and discomfort; gentleness, respect, and affability are positive attitudes promoting a climate (tone) of warmth and joy. The interior manner by which we approach God is of immense importance in prayer. Julian of Norwich writes that when one is comfortable in coming to the Lord, deeper experiences of prayer are possible: "And so prayer makes harmony between God and man's soul, because when man is at ease with God he does not need to pray, but to contemplate reverently what God says."[36]

Important as our tone is, God's manner and attitude are of even greater significance. God's attitude flows from the divine nature, a nature summarized in the word "love." And love's cousins are reverence, wonder, and awe. What mystery here — our God honoring us with graciousness and courtesy. Again the insight of Julian of Norwich captures the tonality of our God: "Of everything which I saw, this was the greatest comfort to me, that our Lord is so familiar and so courteous, and this most filled my soul with delight and surety."[37]

When we enter into prayer, it is of great profit to ask for the Spirit of reverence and wonder, the same Spirit that empowered Jesus as he addressed the Father in silence and solitude. When gifted with these gentle and strong attitudes, our prayer takes on an entirely different quality. Without these gifts our

---

35. Whittaker Chambers, *Witness* (New York: Random House, 1952), 19.

36. *Julian of Norwich: Showings*, trans. from the critical text with an introduction by Edmund Colledge, O.S.A., and James Walsh, S.J. (New York: Paulist Press, 1978), 159.

37. Ibid., 136.

hearts are stifled and our service cool. The reverent feel deeply and serve generously; the awe-filled see with wonder and hear with trembling.

8. God's activity in prayer is more important than our activity.[38]

Prayer is a personal response to God's presence. It is more something that God does to us, rather than anything we do. This means that God first makes Himself present to us. Prayer is our awareness and then response to God.[39]

~

In the first place it should be known that if a person is seeking God, his Beloved is seeking him much more.[40]

~

In prayer we shift the center of living from self-consciousness to self-surrender. God is the center toward which all forces tend. He is the source, and we are the flowing of His force, the ebb and flow of His tides.[41]

Self-sufficiency is much admired in our culture. So deep is this trait that we imagine that nothing happens unless we make it happen. We assume responsibility for the total management of our lives, including the spiritual domain. Control is the goal whereas we are aware of rampant addiction and compulsiveness. With such a mentality, it is not surprising that God's initiatives and graces are unable to penetrate our hearts. We are like a dancer always seeking to lead, suspicious of external influences. The consequences of such a disposition are tragic: "A person extinguishes the spirit by wanting to conduct himself in a way different from that in which God is leading him."[42]

While acknowledging both the necessity and health of self-reliance in its deepest meaning, complete self-motivation leads to stagnation and death. Faith tells us that God always takes the

---

38. See Ps. 138; John 6:44.
39. Fr. Armand Nigro's "Prayer" (source unknown).
40. *The Collected Works of St. John of the Cross*, 620.
41. Abraham Heschel, *Man's Quest for God*, 7.
42. *The Collected Works of St. John of the Cross*, 232.

initiative and that Christian living is basically a response to what God is asking or doing in us. In no way does this detract from the principle that we must make things happen, not just allow things to happen. But that activity is consequent upon the word of God. The Christian heart, informed by wisdom, seeks simply to please God in all things, whatever is asked. Though the request may be shrouded in darkness, though God's ways and thoughts are light years away from our own, the challenge remains the same: "Our task is always the humble and courageous one of listening obediently and acting boldly."[43] Prayerful activity must flow from deep listening to the word of God. The day should begin with a listening disposition; it should end with a review of our responses to God's word.

Prayer is dialogic: a word is spoken in love and answered out of love. The answer itself becomes the substance for the next movement in the dynamic and mutual relationship between God and humankind. The familiarity here is profound if at times stressful; its absence creates an incredible loneliness and a haunting restlessness.

9. *There is no one way of prayer; pluralism in prayer must be carefully guarded and encouraged.*[44]

God leads each one along different paths so that hardly one spirit will be found like another in even half its method or procedure.[45]

~

I do not say this without reason, for, as I have said, it is very important for us to realize that God does not lead us all by the same road, and perhaps she who believes herself to be going along the lowest road is the highest in the Lord's eyes. So it does not follow that, because all of

---

43. Romano Guardini, *The Life of Faith*, trans. John Chapin (Westminster, Md.: Newman Press, 1961), 106.
44. See Col. 3:12–17; Luke 4:42–44.
45. *The Collected Works of St. John of the Cross*, 633.

us in this house practice prayer, we are all *perforce* to be contemplatives.[46]

~

There is no prescribed way to God. God leads men where He will. Always in ways suited to the individual, by taking into account his traits of character and spiritual aspirations, the times and environment in which he lives and by which he is influenced, Providence is already at work.[47]

Uniqueness of personality type helps to specify what form and style of prayer are most appropriate for the individual. God works with and through our individuality. To adopt someone else's manner of prayer can be dangerous and useless. Sheer imitation, without any matching of spiritual blood type, leads to frustration and discouragement. As the saying goes, "Different strokes for different folks!" So too in the spiritual life: different prayer for different persons and circumstances. Prayer is as varied as people, with the commonality arising from the word/response dynamic underlying all communication between God and humans.

Just as prayer varies from one person to the next, there can also be variations of prayer within a single life. During periods of faith development, vocal and formal prayer may well be the best prayer style; at other stages, meditative or contemplative prayer may be in order. To go a step further. Within a single week or even within a given hour of prayer, a variety of forms and communication dynamic may be operative. What is essential is not the form but the experience of God. Prayer is a means to an end, union with God. The paths to union are multiple.

In his haunting novel *Night*, Elie Wiesel writes: "There are a thousand and one gates leading into the orchard of mystical truth. Every human being has his own gate. We must never make the mistake of wanting to enter the orchard by any gate but our own. To do this is dangerous for the one who en-

---

46. *The Complete Works of St. Teresa of Jesus*, 2:307–8.
47. Guardini, *The Life of Faith*, 18.

ters and also for those who are already there."[48] Pluralism is threatened when we imagine that the orchard has but one entrance.

10. *Prayer leads to intimacy with God and to solidarity with all creation.*[49]

In prayer I can enter into contact with the God who created me and all things out of love. In prayer I can find a new sense of belonging since it is there that I am most related.[50]

∼

"At the day of judgement," he [Pope John XXIII] declared, "we won't be asked whether we realized unity, but whether we prayed, worked and suffered for it."[51]

∼

For this reason contemplation is the source of fraternal love. It is essential to have gazed into the features and conduct of incarnate and crucified love in order to make its law a firm support of our wavering love when a decisive situation arises — the law which bids us to bear all things, hope all things, believe all things, and to be patient.[52]

Activities find their meaning in terms of their goals. The ultimate end of the spiritual life is union with God, and by means of that unity we are mysteriously united to all of creation. Oneness is attained by love and prayer is the central love-act in our lives. Through ongoing communication with God, we grow in knowledge, love, and respect until one day we awake to an incredible intimacy that knows no description. The bonding here is subtle and mysterious, powerful and challenging. The Lord stands at the door knocking. Each of us must make a choice.

---

48. Elie Wiesel, *Night* (New York: Avon Books, 1969), 14.

49. See Pss. 139; Jer. 31:31–34.

50. Henri J. M. Nouwen, *The Genesee Diary: Report from a Trappist Monastery* (New York: Doubleday & Co., 1986), 51.

51. Peter Hebblethwaite, *Pope John XXIII: Shepherd of the Modern World* (New York: Doubleday & Company, 1985), 470.

52. Hans Urs von Balthasar, *Prayer*, 172.

Consequent to our *fiat*, God comes to dwell with us and our homes are never the same.

Prayer's unifying power does not terminate in intimacy with God alone. It facilitates a deeper union with our sisters and brothers as well. To be united to God draws us into a more intense bonding with all of creation. The closer we come to the cross of Christ and the nearer to the power of the Spirit, the closer we find ourselves to the source of all life and holiness. Thus, without prayer, alienation and isolation happen, whether they are felt or not. Lack of communication with God means separation from our source and simultaneously a distancing from all aspects of creation. Prayer gives us entrance into the heart of our triune God and into the mystery of God's loving creation.

Because prayer fosters intimacy and solidarity, it is not uncommon for fear to arise within our hearts and souls. Intimacy means vulnerability. To know and to be known completely involves the possibility of rejection. Perhaps we are not convinced that we are lovable. Faith and trust is needed as we approach the mystery of a God, whose mercy is infinite and whose love is extravagant. Humility and courage are the virtues empowering us to draw close to our sisters and brothers, knowing that through grace we can accept them and be accepted by them. Prayer involves revelation, acceptance, and humility; it demands faith, trust, and courage. Gifted by the Spirit, we enter the land of prayer and therein find our peace.

In reflecting upon any aspect of the spiritual life, we must view it contextually. This essay points out ten signs on the road to union through the practice of prayer. A corresponding set of principles regarding other aspects of our life in Christ delineates other paths and seasons of the journey. The map is large because the life of the Spirit embraces all of reality. But whatever the principle or its specification, the destination is always the same: the experience of *Love*. That experience becomes actuality as we move from maps into the lands they describe.

Chapter 2

PRINCIPLES OF DISCERNMENT

The journey of life is filled with many choices, the consequences of which are far-reaching. Decision making need not be a solitary process, though in the end we stand alone in our individual choices. Friends and counselors frequently give helpful advice. We also have the advantage of personal and collective experience from which we can extract patterns and principles that provide wisdom and guidance. This essay spells out ten principles that can help us discern God's voice and respond to the Lord's call with courage and generosity. A basic assumption underlies this endeavor: growth is more likely to happen when we reflect critically upon our experience and note reoccurring patterns than if we move from one spontaneous experience to another without dealing explicitly with any of them. Reflection, done in prayer and with serious intent, provides insight and energy for spiritual development. Growth in the Lord is impeded with reflection and articulation are absent.

The following methodology will be used: (1) the *articulation* of ten principles of discernment; (2) a series of *quotations* from various authors who reflect some dimension of each principle; (3) a tripartite *commentary*, which includes a reference to Scripture, an *image* illustrating the principle, and an *exam-*

ple from literature (plays, movies, etc.) providing a case study of the theme.

Discernment is a gift to be exercised. Principles are abstractions offering meaning. Both are significant for human and spiritual growth. This essay presents the principles; the reader brings the gift and the experience. The hope is that the roads intersect rather than run parallel.

1. Discernment is a prayerful process by which experiences are interpreted in faith.

By discernment of spirits is meant the process by which we examine, in the light of faith and in the connaturality of love, the nature of the spiritual states we experience in ourselves and in others. The purpose of such examination is to decide, as far as possible, which of the movements we experience lead to the Lord and to a more perfect service of him and our brothers, and which deflect us from this goal.[1]

~

Basically, as I see it, *discernment* may be defined as the meeting point of prayer and action. This is, discernment is the art of recognizing what God is asking of us — what he would like us to do with our lives, how he wishes us to respond to the concrete life-situations which we encounter in following our vocation.[2]

~

The Christian who reflects on his own experience and on that of the community, who seeks to discern in these the divine voice, and who wants to respond to it by redirecting his life, is — theologically speaking — engaged in prayer.[3]

1. Edward Malatesta, *Discernment of Spirit*, (Collegeville, Minn.: Liturgical Press, 1970), 9.

2. Thomas H. Greene, S.J., *Darkness in the Marketplace* (Notre Dame, Ind.: Ave Maria Press, 1982), 69.

3. Gregory Baum, *Man Becoming* (New York: Herder and Herder, 1970), 256.

"Then he [Jesus] bent down and wrote on the ground again" (John 8:8). The adulterous woman stood before him; the scribes and pharisees made their accusations; the people observed with keen curiosity. We do not know exactly what transpired in the mind and heart of Jesus as he leaned forward and wrote in the sand with his finger. We do know that this crisis situation needed an interpretation. Jesus was a prayerful person; his bending forward in silence may well have been a deep moment of communion with the Father. We do know the Lord's response to the situation: the accusers could silently withdraw, the accused could depart without condemnation. This is but one example of Jesus' ministry. In many other situations he turned explicitly to the Father for guidance: the mountain prayer before choosing the disciples, the garden prayer before his obedient acceptance of death, the desert prayer when tempted to infidelity. The necessity for discernment arises from crossroad experiences; the standard for discernment is whether or not the decision leads to God and to more complete service; the act of discernment requires the posture of contemplative prayer.

The *combine* is used in harvesting and threshing grain. It separates the grain from the straw, retaining the former for winter feeding and discharging the latter in neat rows. The wheat and the chaff, the good and the evil, the true and the false, the beautiful and the ugly — throughout history the human spirit has sought to distinguish one from the other, even in periods of relativism. This is no simple process. The gray areas are far ranging, time is often needed and simply not available, the multiplicity of experiences clogs up our discerning minds and hearts. Despite these obstacles, the spiritual combine of a discerning heart must perform its duty as well as it can. With some prayer, learning, and guidance, the spirits of good and evil can be detected and responded to in appropriate ways.

Graham Greene's *The Power and the Glory* is a story about spiritual discernment, its successes and its failures. The "whiskey priest" must constantly make decisions regarding himself and his ministry in the midst of a Mexican religious persecution. The failure to discern well may be grounded in this reflection: "a prayer demanded an act and he had no intention of acting." Successful discernment demands courage and sanctity:

> He felt only an immense disappointment because he had to go to God empty-handed, with nothing done at all. It seemed to him at that moment that it would have been quite easy to have been a saint. It would only have needed a little self-restraint and a little courage. He felt like someone who has missed happiness by seconds at an appointed place. He knew now that at the end there was only one thing that counted — to be a saint.[4]

Discernment is that prayerful process enabling each individual and the larger community to move in the direction of sanctity.

2. Discernment must deal with many voices seeking to capture our minds, hearts, and energies.

> Since the mysterious voice of the Spirit is not the only voice we hear but comes to us accompanied by the tumultuous sounds of our own conflicting impulses and the clamorings of the entire creation, it is essential for us to be able to *discern* the presence of the Spirit in order to choose to say "yes" to him.[5]

~

> So the soul that waits in silence must learn to disentangle the voice of God from the net of other voices — the ghostly whisperings of the subconscious self, the luring voices of the world, the hindering voices of misguided friendship, the clamor of personal ambition and vanity, the murmur of self-will, the song of unbridled imagination, the thrilling note of religious romance. To learn to keep one's ear true to so subtle a labyrinth of spiritual

---

4. Graham Greene, *The Power and the Glory* (New York: Viking Press, 1940), 284.

5. *Discernment of Spirits*, 9.

sound is indeed at once a great adventure and a liberal education. One hour of such listening may give us a deeper insight into the mysteries of human nature, and surer instinct for divine values, than a year's hard study or external intercourse with men.[6]

~

While his mind had been pursuing its intangible phantoms, and turning in irresolution from such pursuit, he had heard about him the constant voices of his father and of his masters, urging him to be a gentleman above all things and urging him to be a good Catholic above all things. These voices had now come to hollow sounding in his ear. When the gymnasium had been opened he had heard another voice urging him to be strong and manly and healthy and when the movement towards national revival had begun to be felt in the college, yet another voice had bidden him to be true to his country and help to raise up her language and tradition. In the profane world, as he foresaw, a worldly voice would bid him raise up his father's fallen state by his labors and, meanwhile, the voice of his school comrades urged him to be a decent fellow, to shield others from blame or to beg them off and to do his best to get free days for the school. And it was the din of all these hollow sounding voices that made him halt irresolutely in the pursuit of phantoms. He gave them ear only for a time but he was happy only when he was far from them, beyond their call, alone or in the company of phantasmal comrades.[7]

The parable of the good shepherd stresses the importance of recognizing the voice of the master (John 10:1–5). Eternal life depends upon this. Only those who hear and respond to God's will will enter into the fullness of life. Yet Jesus, the good

---

6. Hermann Hesse, *Steppenwolf* (New York: Holt, Rinehart and Winston, 1963), 43.
7. James Joyce, *A Portrait of the Artist as a Young Man* (New York: Colonial Press, 1944), 83–84.

shepherd, was one voice among many. Competition for the mind and heart of the sheep was great and, given the gift of freedom, there could be no forcing of individual liberty. Some people that Jesus called refused to follow: the rich young man, Judas, the scribes and pharisees. Others heard the loving call and became committed disciples: John, Stephen, Magdalene, Paul. The voice of the risen shepherd, once slain, continues to compete with the sounds of our time. He can be heard in our sacraments of faith, in the sights and sounds of nature, in the revelation of Scripture, in the community of believers, in the teaching of the church, in the words and deeds of our fellow pilgrims. Life itself is a summons to reach out and fulfill our task of becoming fully human in order that we might glorify God.

The *tuner* on the radio allows us to select a desired station. The possibilities are many: beautiful or dissonant music, intelligent or banal conversation, candid or deceitful advertisements. With a twist of the dial we have power to enter or exit various environments and with that choice to expose ourselves to ideas and images that shape our lives. In the spiritual realm, the gift of discernment tunes us into God's invitations and demands. The divine voice will both comfort and confront us if we dare to listen.

Chaim Potok's novel *My Name Is Asher Lev* presents an artistically gifted young man who has to discern among many voices. Early in life Asher Lev recognizes that his ability to draw has the potential for self-fulfillment while simultaneously presenting the danger of seriously rupturing his relationship with his parents and the Jewish community. In anger and confusion he addresses God:

> You don't want me to use the gift; why did you give it to me? Or did it come from the Other Side? It was horrifying to think my gift may have been given to me by the source of evil and ugliness. How can evil and ugliness make a gift of beauty?[8]

---

8. Chaim Potok, *My Name Is Asher Lev* (New York: Fawcett Crest Books, 1972), 116.

The pressure from the leaders of the community, the warnings of friends, the intrinsic urging of the gift, the delicate relationship with his parents were all voices seeking attention and action. Would the gift be heard and exercised regardless of the cost? Discernment calls for radical fidelity to God, self, and others. Wisdom and courage are needed to hear the truth and implement it in our personal history.

3. Discernment is cultivated in listening love that allows one to hear the felt-experience of good and evil movements within oneself, others, and society.

> For these souls, their hearts tell them what God desires. They have only to listen to the promptings of their heart to interpret his will in the existing circumstances. God's plans, disguised as they are, reveal themselves to us through our intuition rather than through our reason.[9]

~

> Love gives freedom. Love accepts another person as he is, and discerns in the other person hidden strength. Love communicates to the other a new kind of self-possession, and enables the other to act with self-confidence.[10]

~

> Only by the supernatural working of grace can a soul pass through its own annihilation to be the place where alone it can get the sort of attention which can attend to truth and to affliction. It is the same attention which listens to both of them. The name of this intense, pure, disinterested, gratuitous, generous attention is love.[11]

~

> It is not blind love that is enduring love, the love that God himself is. It is a seeing love, a knowing love, a love that looks through into the depth of the heart of God, and into

---

9. Jean Pierre De Caussade, *Abandonment to Divine Providence* (New York: Doubleday Image, 1975), 105.

10. Baum, *Man Becoming*, 50.

11. George A. Panichas, ed. *The Simone Weil Reader* (New York: David McKay Company, 1977), 333.

the depth of our hearts. There is no strangeness to love; it is the only power to complete and lasting knowledge.[12]

Jesus was a listener and a lover (Matt. 16:13–23). In a powerful exchange with Peter, Jesus listens to Peter's profession that his master is the Messiah. Jesus also hears Peter's unwillingness to embrace the harsh fact that the Messiah must suffer and die. As he listens with love, Jesus discerns the first response of Peter as coming from the Father and the second movement and response as coming from mere human standards and desires. The striking example of double discernment resonates with many of our own experiences in which we act out of mixed motives and according to diverse and sometimes contradictory criteria. Authentic discernment is possible only when one has the graced ability to listen in love to the deepest impulses, urges, and longings of the human heart with great care and exquisite respect. Jesus models for us the very essence of discernment.

The *sunflower* delights both our eye and imagination. In the morning the golden flower faces the east, awaiting the dawn; by evening it gazes to the west as though pursuing a god. Two qualities are evident in this docile plant: a "listening" power that enables it to take in the sun's warm rays and its ability to respond to the brilliance of the sun's light. This image highlights the importance of sensitivity in the discernment process. The slightest impulse, urging, or prompting must be absorbed and processed to see whether or not it comes from the Master. That listening and processing is grounded in love. Love pulls us out of self-preoccupation and the narrow confines of our parochialism. The sunflower images a type of listening and love characteristic of a discerning heart. Would that the simplicity, spontaneity, docility, and flexibility of the sunflower were ours!

The movie *Ordinary People* presented a scene in which an emotionally disturbed young man reached out to a psychiatrist for help. Initially the relationship between the doctor and youth did not go well. Later, with time and patience, the deep

---

12. Paul Tillich, *The Shaking of the Foundations* (New York: Charles Scribner's Sons, 1948), 110.

loving concern and intense listening by the doctor won out. The boy revealed his burden and the healing process began. More than simple listening transpired here: a deep discernment of the movements of the heart surfaced, were owned, and were dealt with. More than superficial concern was demonstrated here: a profound, radical trust resulted in the giving of life and well-being. In this exchange between patient and doctor heart spoke to heart (*cor ad cor*) and even though religious language is not used, it is obvious that the grace of discernment is operative. Anyone with faith can recognize it immediately.

4. Discernment relies on two foundations: Jesus and revelation.

The disciple living today...does possess one ultimate criterion for correct discernment: i.e., Jesus himself.[13]

~

With the help of the Holy Spirit, it is the task of the entire people of God, especially pastors and theologians, to hear, distinguish and interpret the many voices of our age, and to judge them in the light of the divine word. In this way, revealed truth can always be more deeply penetrated, better understood, and set forth to greater advantage.[14]

~

Jesus is our master to whom we do not pay enough attention. He speaks to every heart and utters the word of life, the essential word for each of us, but we do not hear it. We would like to know what he has said to other people, yet we do not listen to what he says to us.[15]

An example of discernment can be found in the miracle of the loaves (John 6:1–71). Many of the disciples who had followed Jesus up to his point now walked away, finding incredible the claim that Jesus himself was the bread of life. The

13. Jon Sobrino, *Christology at the Crossroads*, trans. John Drury (Maryknoll, N.Y.: Orbis Books, 1978), 129.
14. "Gaudium et Spes," *The Documents of Vatican II* (New York: Herder and Herder, 1966), 246.
15. Jean Pierre De Caussade, *Abandonment to Divine Providence*, 53.

Lord turned to the Twelve and asked if they too would go away. Simon Peter's response: "Lord, to whom shall we go? You have the words of eternal life" (John 6:68). Peter's specific choice to remain with the Lord was based on the person of Christ and on his word. No abstract philosophy here; no esoteric theology; no subtle psychology. Discernment flowed from a relationship of trust and faith. Implicit in such a discernment process is fidelity: decisions are made in terms of personal commitment. Thus, "discernment enters in not at the level of principle but at the consequent level of concrete action — of specific decisions by souls committed to live by the principles given by the Lord too guide the Christian life."[16]

The *keystone* of an arch is in a precarious position. Its presence makes the arch integral, but it is dependent on the two columns that it unites. If either column is missing there simply is no arch, and the stone meant to be a key remains just an ordinary stone. Christian discernment rests on the personal column of Jesus Christ: his values and affections are the very substance we use in sorting out the many options of life. Discernment also rests on Sacred Scripture, which provides a vision of salvation history and the backdrop against which we measure what is of God and what is not. Blessed are the poor, the peacemakers, the ones who hunger and thirst for justice; ungodly are the self-indulgent, the self-serving, the lukewarm. Revelation clarifies which actions are life-giving and those which lead to death. The person of Jesus leaves unambiguous the path we are to follow. The keystone in the arch of discernment stands firm when supported by Scripture and the Word of God.[17]

---

16. Green, *Darkness in the Marketplace*, 70.

17. Switching metaphors from keystone to a royal road, another dimension of discernment is offered by John Cassian: "Lacking the training provided by older men they could in no way acquire this virtue of discernment which, avoiding extremes, teaches the monk to walk always on the royal road. It keeps him from veering to the right, that is, it keeps him from going with stupid presumption and excessive fervor beyond the boundary of reasonable restraint. It keeps him from going to the left to carelessness and sin, to sluggishness of spirit, and all this on the pretext of actually keeping the body under control" (John Cassian, *Conferences*,

In his famous *Confessions*, St. Augustine tells of the importance of God's word and the person of Jesus in his life. Reading
a passage in St. Paul's letter to the Romans, the future bishop of
Hippo was overwhelmed by God's word. Although Augustine's
hunger for truth was nourished by philosophy, it was Scripture
that became pivotal in his life. And Jesus became the object of
Augustine's deep affectivity, a love that once frantically sought
fulfillment in unbridled sensuality. With these two sources it
is no wonder that Augustine became a keen, incisive decision-
maker. Both as a judge of human affairs and as an exegete of
God's word, he brought justice and life to many because his
process of discernment was rooted in the Lord and in biblical
faith.

5. Discernment assumes that God is continually working in the depth of every individual and community.

He [God] revealed himself several times reigning, as is
said before, but principally in man's soul; he has taken
there his resting place and his honorable city. Out of this
honorable throne he will never rise or depart without
end. Marvelous and splendid is the place where the Lord
dwells; and therefore he wants us promptly to attend to
the touching of his grace, rejoicing more in his unbroken
love than sorrowing over our frequent fallings.[18]

~

But whatever we do, we do it because we are drawn to
this particular action without knowing why. All we can say
can be reduced to this: "I feel drawn to write, to read, to
question and examine. I obey this feeling, and God who is
responsible for it thus builds up within me a kind of spiritual store which, in the future, will develop into a core of
usefulness for myself and for others." This is what makes
it essential for us to be simple-hearted, gentle, compli-

---

trans. and preface by Colm Luibheid with introduction by Owen Chadwick [New
York: Paulist Press, 1985], 62).

18. Julian of Norwich: *Showings*, trans. Edmund Colledge, O.S.A., and James
Walsh, S.J., Classics of Western Spirituality (New York: Paulist Press, 1978), 337.

ant and sensitive to the slightest breath of these almost
imperceptible promptings.[19]

~

Ah, but it is hard to find this track of the divine in the
midst of this life we lead, in this besotted humdrum age
of spiritual blindness, with its architecture, its business,
its politics, its men.[20]

~

The realization that God is active in all that happens at
every moment is the deepest knowledge we can have in
this life of the things of God.[21]

Creation is God's presence to us in beauty; the cross is
God's presence to us in our brokenness and twistedness.[22]
God's creative and redemptive work is at work wherever there
is life. Whether or not a given individual responds to that
presence is contingent upon one's cooperation with grace
and the proper use of freedom. The point is: God is always working (John 6). John's Gospel drives this faith fact
home. When accepted, we are challenged to become increasingly conscious of divine stirrings deep within ourselves and
our communities. Focal awareness, a high intensity of consciousness, may not be all that frequent, but a subsidiary
awareness, a sense of background presence, can become a
way of life.[23] As our faith deepens we become ever more

---

19. De Caussade, *Abandonment to Divine Providence*, 81.

20. Hesse, *Steppenwolf*, 35.

21. De Caussade, *Abandonment to Divine Providence*, 117.

22. John Shea, *Stories of God: An Unauthorized Biography* (Chicago: Thomas
More Association, 1978), 152.

23. In an essay entitled *The Study of Man*, Michael Polanyi writes: "We may say
that when we comprehend a particular set of items as parts of a whole, the focus
of our attention is shifted from the hitherto uncomprehended particulars to the
understanding of their joint meaning. This shift of attention does not make us
lose sight of the particulars, since one can see a whole only by seeing its parts,
but it changes altogether the manner in which we are aware of the particulars. We
become aware of them now in terms of the whole on which we have fixed our
attention. I shall call this a *subsidiary awareness* of the particulars, by contrast to
a *focal awareness* which would fix attention on the particulars in themselves, and
not as parts of the whole" (*The Study of Man* [Chicago: University of Chicago Press,
1959], 29–30).

sensitive to the working of God's Spirit in our minds and hearts.

One of the small miracles in life is the process by which the vineyard captures the sun's rays and the nutrients of nature to transform them into grapes. Upon being harvested and crushed, grapes enter the *fermentation* process. Through the hidden workings of bacteria plus proper temperature, darkness, and sugars, the grapes are converted into wine. Our spiritual journey involves a similar process of ongoing conversion, fermentation, change. The sourness of the unredeemed areas of our inner life is turned, by God's grace and mercy, into the nourishing wine that sustains and enriches our lives.

In her sensitive allegory *Hinds' Feet on High Places*, Hannah Hurnard shares with us the fermentation process of Much-Afraid, the main character of the story who eventually becomes "much-trust." At first the heroine is enslaved by fear, oppressed by human respect, devoid of joy. Gradually she begins to sense and respond to the stirrings of grace within her soul. God's promptings led Much-Afraid into freedom, then acts of courage. Her story is symbolic of all those held bondage by fear. One of the reasons for her liberation and growth in God's will was a daily exercise that we might all heed:

> To this place [a well] she was in the habit of going early every morning to meet Him and learn His wishes and commands for the day, and again in the evening to give her report on the day's work.[24]

Such conversation and accountability enrich the discerning heart.

---

24. Hannah Hurnard, *Hinds' Feet on High Places* (Old Tappan, N.J.: Fleming H. Revell Company, 1973), 13.

6. Discernment respects the nature of time and is willing to wait freely for a decision that has need of clarification, detachment, and magnanimity.

The poet contrasts us in our waiting and in our going ahead. For those who take initiative into their own hands, either in the atheism of pride or in the atheism of despair, the words are weary, faint, and exhausted. The inverse comes with waiting: renewed strength, mounting up, running, walking. But that is in waiting. It is in receiving and not grasping, in inheriting and not possessing, in praising and not seizing. It is in knowing that initiative has passed from our hands and we are safer for it.[25]

~

Lightning and thunder requires time, the light of stars require time, deeds require time even after they are done, before they can be seen and heard.[26]

~

Simply by making us wait he [God] increases our desire, which in turn enlarges the capacity of our soul, making it able to receive what is to be given us.[27]

Many of Jesus' parables deal with the experience of time and waiting (Luke 12:35–40). One tells of the necessity of being ready to greet the master at the time of the wedding feast. Happy are those who are awake and prepared for that coming. By contrast, fear, weariness, and even impatience are dispositions that are not conducive to hearing and responding to God's unexpected comings. Milton's "they also serve who only stand and wait" characterizes true discipleship. Timing in decision making is subtle and delicate. God's time (*kairos*) is different from human time (*chronos*). Acting out of season, the season of grace, is not healthy. A basic guideline in terms of

---

25. Walter Brueggemann, *The Prophetic Imagination* (Philadelphia: Fortress Press, 1978), 78–79.

26. Peter Berger, *A Rumor of Angels* (New York: Doubleday & Company, 1969), 11.

27. Thomas H. Green, S.J., *When the Well Runs Dry* (Notre Dame: Ave Maria Press, 1979), 113.

time and waiting is the following: "act on your clarities." When things are muddy we wait, however painful that may be. Without expecting a certitude or clarity that is unrealistic, we must gradually become comfortable with seeking and waiting until God's will is manifest. Once that happens, hesitation becomes sinful.

If we *dial* a specific number, the telephone company informs us of the current temperature and time. Would that the exact climate and timing of our inner seasons were as easily known. It is difficult to discern the exact time and climate of the soul's environment. Yet some guidelines are clear. Decisions of major importance should not be made during times of depression. Nor should significant choices be made when romanticism sweeps through the heart, blinding us to larger responsibilities. We discern on level ground, not on the peaks nor in the valleys. The correct time (and space) is known more through intuition than discursive thought; we sense our way through the field of discernment rather than figure it out. A phone call may locate us and orientate us in reference to the sun; discernment provides a bearing in reference to a much brighter Light.

Shakespeare's *King Lear* provides a case study of timing and discernment. As Lear was aging, he decided to distribute his property and wealth among his three daughters, giving each a share in proportion to her profession of love for her father, the king. Not only was Lear unwise in his standard for division, he was totally misguided in terms of timing. You don't distribute your wealth or power, even to daughters or sons, until one foot is solidly in the grave. The consequence of Lear's poor discernment was insanity and death. Life-giving discernment demands a standard, one based on knowledge of reality, the way things really are. Lear lacked that standard and suffered severely from his misjudgment. Though apparently magnanimous, Lear was less wise than the fool in the play. Shakespeare has much to teach us, even if through negative examples, of the nature of discernment.

7. Discernment is a gift (grace) given to those who are
properly disposed to receive it because of obedience and
surrender.

The hearing of God's Word requires complete self-
surrender.[28]

~

In everything else, the soul will preserve a perfect liberty,
always ready to obey the stirrings of grace the moment it
becomes aware of them, and to surrender to the care of
providence.[29]

~

I don't know Who — or what — put the question, I don't
know when it was put. I don't even remember answer-
ing. But at some moment I did answer Yes to someone —
to Something — and from that hour I was certain that
existence is meaningful and that, therefore, my life in
self-surrender had a goal.[30]

The Annunciation narrative tells of Mary's perplexing situation (Luke 1:26–38). Her future with Joseph had been determined. Plans were made and important decisions set in
motion. Suddenly God breaks into the "best-laid schemes o'
mice an' men." How to respond to this unexpected visitation?
To whom should one listen? How could one be certain that
this was the call of God? This biblical account gives us a classic example of discernment's dilemma, the tension between
our plans and God's will. The divine will summons and history hangs in balance. Though struggling with fear and the
unknown, Mary discerned the voice of God and, in humble
obedience and generous surrender, committed her life to the
providence of God. Mary's gift of discernment was grounded
in her identity as the Lord's handmaid. Mary knew who she

---

28. *Meister Eckhart*, trans. Raymond B. Blakney (New York: Harper Torchbooks, 1941), 33.

29. De Caussade, *Abandonment to Divine Providence*, 88.

30. Dag Hammarskjold, *Markings*, trans. Leif Sjoberg and W. H. Auden (New York: Alfred A. Knopf, 1966), 205.

was, and out of that self-knowledge she responded totally and extravagantly to God's stirrings.

Technology has provided people who have impaired hearing with *hearing aids* that sustain or restore the world of sound. Where before there was deafness, now there is the possibility of hearing and responding to the various voices that are heard. Physical listening has its counterpart in the spiritual realm, as does deafness. Often we do not hear. At times, we choose not to listen; on other occasions, some circumstance blocks us from hearing. Whatever the cause of deafness, we fail to discern the words and movements of the Lord because the gift of discernment has not been activated. Hearing aids can be adjusted, even turned off. When God asks what is demanding or unpleasant we have the option of disregarding the summons. Thus, the discernment process has the quality of mutuality: the call and gift from God, the free response of obedience and surrender from the human person. In this mutuality, God respects our freedom too much to force a response. Further, God does not withhold this gift from anyone, since it is a grace that determines destinies. If discernment is not operative, it is because the gift offered was rejected or never exercised.

The autobiography of St. Thérèse of Lisieux, *Story of a Soul*, is a candid revelation of a deep love relationship. Surrender and obedience were qualities that gave constant direction to the saint's life. These dispositions opened her to a life of discernment. Thérèse realized that Christian living demanded not only recognition of what is to be done but the actual doing. She writes: "As little birds learn to sing by listening to their parents, so children learn the science of virtue, the sublime song of Divine Love from souls responsible for forming them."[31] Authentic discernment moves from listening to virtue. God uses many intermediaries (parents, teachers, friends, "enemies") to both proclaim his message and model for us a response. In this environment the gift of discernment takes root. Thérèse's be-

---

31. *Story of a Soul: The Autobiography of St. Therese of Lisieux*, trans. John Clarke, O.C.D. (Washington, D.C.: ICS Publications, 1975), 113.

ing was receptive to the stirrings of grace. The song of divine love was heard; the refrain was also a melody of deep love.

8. Discernment blends faith and pragmatism: it searches out God's will in radical trust and does it.

The People of God believes that it is led by the Spirit of the Lord, who fills the earth. Motivated by this faith, it labors to decipher authentic signs of God's presence and purpose in the happenings, needs, and desires in which this People has a part along with other men of our age. For faith throws a new light on everything, manifests God's design for man's total vocation, and thus directs the mind to solutions which are fully human.[32]

~

The will certainly seems to me to be united in some way to the will of God; but it is by the effects of this prayer and the actions which follow it that the genuineness of the experience must be tested and there is no better crucible for doing so than this.[33]

~

Every activity is related to good and evil twice over: by its performance and by its principle.[34]

While teaching one day, Jesus was interrupted when some men, carrying their paralyzed friend to where Jesus was, ingeniously lowered their ill friend through the roof (Luke 5:17–26). The story is familiar. Two things should be noted for our purpose. First, these men had a deep faith in the healing power of Jesus. Second, their faith was active as they expended much energy and took considerable risk in endeavoring to get their friend into the presence of Christ. Their trust and courage

---

32. "Pastoral Constitution on the Church in the Modern World," *The Documents of Vatican II*, Walter M. Abbott, S.J., general editor (New York: Herder and Herder, 1966), 209, no. 11.

33. *The Complete Works of St. Teresa of Jesus*, ed. and trans. E. Allison Peers (London: Sheed & Ward, 1944), 2:238.

34. *The Simone Weil Reader*, 292.

were rewarded in the healing and forgiveness of their paralyzed friend.

Discernment is both relational and functional, contemplative and active, faith-filled and pragmatic. No dichotomy exists within the spiritual life between our belief in God and our love for our sisters and brothers. True discernment involves integration so that action will always be subsequent to our faith in God. Discernment will call us forth to be agents of change.

H_2O is the chemical formula describing our precious gift of water. The blending of these two elements produces a substance necessary for human existence. Hydrogen without oxygen fails to give us our refreshing liquid and vice versa. So too in the spiritual domain: faith without action is dead; acting without faith loses its ultimate significance. The wellspring and fountain of the spiritual life is the grace of discernment, a life-giving mixture of faith and deed. Depending upon the developmental phases of the community or individual, the weight will shift more toward faith, more toward action during the different seasons of our life. Though similar to the laws of nature, our spiritual dynamics are much more subtle but no less real.

Dag Hammarskjold's journal, *Markings*, records the diverse movements of his inner life. Hammarskjold, busy with international affairs and with the multiple responsibilities of the United Nations, took time to nurture and develop his interior life. Often he speaks of faith and its relationship to action. One passage will suffice:

> We act in faith — and miracles occur. In consequence, we are tempted to make the miracles the ground of our faith. The cost of such weakness is that we lose the confidence of faith. Faith is, faith creates, faith carries. It is not derived from, nor created, nor carried by anything except its own reality.[35]

---

35. Dag Hammarskjold, *Markings*, 145.

The mixture is right: the life embedded in the roots of the tree blossoms forth through the branches, carrying and bringing much nourishment to all who come to be fed.

9. Discernment looks to consequences for its authenticity: decisions are of God if ultimately they lead to life and love.

I am quite sure that no one will be deceived in this way for long if he has a gift for the discernment of spirits and if the Lord has given him true humility: such a person will judge these spirits by their fruits and their resolutions and their love.[36]

~

To estimate the worth of a spiritual decision, we thus have three criteria at our disposal: the authenticity of our union with God, the unity of the different elements of our being, the cohesion which our action assumes in relation to ourselves, to others and to the world.[37]

~

The work of love not only heals the roots of sin, but nurtures practical goodness. When it is authentic you will be sensitive to every need and respond with a generosity unspoiled by selfish intent. Anything you attempt to do without this love will certainly be imperfect, for it is sure to be marred by ulterior motives.[38]

Authentic Christian living results in active and explicit concern for the well-being of others. Jesus draws our attention to the fig tree that is rich in foliage but devoid of fruit (Mark 11:12–14). For a hungry person the fruitless fig tree is worthless. We discern the tree's worth by whether or not it achieves its essential destiny. In our spiritual journey, discernment is tested by the effects of our action and the concomitant affectivity that flows from personal behavior. Does this particular action, here

---

36. *The Complete Works of St. Teresa of Jesus*, 1:378.

37. François Roustang, S.J., *Growth in the Spirit*, trans. Kathleen Pond (New York: Sheed & Ward, 1966), 122.

38. William Johnston, ed., *The Cloud of Unknowning and the Book of Privy Counseling* (New York: Doubleday Image, 1973), 64.

and now, give life, i.e., does it foster an increase of love, joy, and peace? Or does this specific choice in time and space lead to death, i.e., apathy, sadness, and anxiety? Discernment registers at the deepest level of our humanity — in our guts! We must learn to sequester that which nurtures from that which enervates. As in economic affairs so in spiritual matters we come to the bottom line: the financial world turns to profit as the spiritual world looks to life, life to the full.

The *stethoscope* allows medical personnel to listen in on the inner physiological movements of the patient. The trained ear can distinguish proper functionings from pathological disturbances of vital organs. What the naked eye fails to see, the ear with the aid of stethoscope can ascertain. Discernment is a process of listening to the stirrings of many different spirits (impulses, urges, tendencies, whispers, stirrings, movements, etc.) constantly at work within the complexity of our lives. A good spiritual director intuitively senses how our lifestyle and motivational energies impact on the inner terrain. If congruence is sensed, God's word is taking root and bearing much fruit. If there is dissonance, then dialogue (and probably repentance) is in order to understand and remove the disorder. This is no easy task, though a possible one. The movements of the spirit are mixed and often ambiguous. At times, God's word will cause initial disharmony while the work of the evil spirit will simulate order. These uncharted waters make us hesitate and call out for help from a good spiritual navigator.

Sophie's Choice, a novel by William Styron, narrates the many decisions that a young woman had to make in very dire circumstances. Sophie's "choice" was to decide whether or not her young son or daughter would be sent to the gas chamber. Throughout the novel we witness people making choices and dealing with the powerful effects that shape their destinies. These effects basically fall on one or other side of the line: life or death. Unfortunately, many decisions were not life-affirming. Any good story or novel is essentially a study of discernment from an existential point of view. Situations arise, choices are made, life or death follows. No one is exempt from dealing with

the script of his or her own life. The process is universal. Grace
is necessary if we are to discern wisely and act with courage.

10. Discernment leads to truth and, through truth, into freedom.

The very word "truth" filled my heart with enthusiasm.
The beauty of the word shone in my eyes like a spiritual
sun dispelling all shadows — those of ignorance, or error, of deceit, even those of iniquity, which is an error of
measure and a life. "Knowing the truth" — a pleonasm.
With truth there is already knowing, as there is reality and
being. To think the word "truth" is to assume a spiritual
faculty, in which alone truth can be found. It is to assume
the capacity of such a spiritual faculty to conform itself
to being, to reality, in order within itself to produce the
truth. It is also to raise the question of knowing whether
such a faculty exists.[39]

~

And if a will of iron represents one aspect of the liber-
ated soul, flexibility and detachment of spirit represent a
complementary aspect. To obey the inspirations of grace
moment by moment, to adjust oneself readily to the
promptings of a living Master, is a task which demands the
glorious liberty that is the high prerogative of the sons of
God.[40]

~

But at this moment I came upon myself. Previously I had
existed, too, but everything had merely happened to me.
Now I happened to myself. Now I knew: I am myself now,
now I exist. Previously I had been willed to do this or that;
now I willed.[41]

---

39. Raïssa Maritain, *We Have Been Friends Together* (New York: Green and Co.,
1942), 80.
40. E. Herman, *Creative Prayer* (Cincinnati: Forward Movement Publications,
n.d.), 79.
41. C. G. Jung, *Memories, Dreams, Reflections*, ed. Aniela Jaffe, and trans.
Richard and Clara Winston (New York: Vintage Books, 1965), 32–33.

God's word calls us to truth and freedom. Mary Magdalene wandered in the garden in deep dejection because her master and friend was dead (John 20:11–18). Death appeared to have had the final say, leaving Mary with fear and depression. Then the experience of the Lord! The truth is exposed: sin and death are overcome by the cross and resurrection. God's fidelity and power are everlasting. The bond of sin is broken; the sting of death, destroyed. With this truth came freedom, a freedom overflowing with joy. Mary sees and is able to act. This narrative helps us to understand how discernment brings vision and responsibility. In recognizing the risen Lord we come into contact with reality; in being graced, we become gracious. Through the word of God we deepen our sense of identity and mission. This process allows us to find meaning, which allows for motivation, enabling us to risk the use of time and energy in new and creative ways. For Mary Magdalene, Jesus was the truth that leads to freedom; for Mary, his person enabled proper discernment.

Scientists use two instruments in their work of discovery and invention that are, by nature, tools of scientific discernment, the *microscope* and the *telescope*. With awe and wonder, we use the microscope to probe cellular structures, revealing the patterns of life; with anticipation and excitement, we aim our telescopes at the galaxies and see marvels undreamt of by our ancestors. Gifted with such tools we come to know invisible worlds and incredible spaces. The spiritual realm is no less astounding. With the tools of subtle interior silence and perceptive wisdom we scan God's vast plan of creative love. Such dispositions (our supernatural microscope and telescope) are crucial in coming to know truth and to exercise freedom. Discernment falters amid noises; it is blinded and cannot know what is pleasing to God. Discernment is seeing, a seeing that leads to doing the truth in love.

Lavrans Bjorgulfson, speaking of his wife, says: "I know not. You are so strange — and all you have said tonight. I was afraid, Ragnfrid. Like enough I understand not the hearts of women. . . . "[42] In Sigrid Undset's *Kristin Lavransdatter*, we witness the tragedy of ignorance and the paralyzing power of fear that follows from such blindness. Lavrans, a good man, does not understand the heart of his wife, Ragnfrid, nor that of his daughter, Kristin. Their loves were mysterious to him and, lacking proper discernment of their hearts, the tortuous pain of misunderstanding was bound to follow. The truth of the heart is a special knowledge all its own. Only when the heart is "informed" and well-known do the waters of freedom flow.

Principles transcend the particulars of life. Helpful as they might be, life is lived in experience, not reflection. Yet we need to step back ever so often for perspective and meaning. This essay made that attempt.

---

42. Sigrid Undset, *Kristin Lavransdatter*, I *The Bridal Wreath*, trans. Charles Archer and J. C. Scott (New York: Bantam Books, 1976), 232.

Chapter 3

PRINCIPLES OF ASCETICISM

The gospel's call is to full life (John 10:10). That vocation implies that all followers of Christ will journey with him on the road of prayer, almsgiving (service), and fasting. Herein is the fundamental structure of the spiritual life: relating to God through dialogue and presence, relating to our sisters and brothers through an exchange of gifts, relating to ourselves through a discipline that promotes and protects our truest self. Discipleship is therefore relational and experiential. It is a commitment in which a master concern, the Lordship of Jesus, governs all else. That commitment necessitates asceticism.

The ascetical aspect of Christian living has never been popular among the masses. By nature we tend to shy away from deprivation and suffering. Because of the influence of our culture, one of self-gratification, we push asceticism to the margins of our life. This disregard is a tragic loss because with it goes a means of liberation, a gateway to compassion, a witness that the world needs so badly. With the demise of ascetical practices (as with the demise of metaphysics) comes the experience of dissipation and its offspring: fatigue, affliction, darkness, defilement, and weakness. St. John of the Cross has documented this reality in his writings.

At first glance asceticism seems opposed to full life. Even a sister word, "mortification," whispers of suffering and death,

and how can these harsh realities bring about fuller existence? Thus, we must ponder the paradox that the lack of
self-denial inhibits quality of life. In its own strange way, asceticism makes us hunger for truth, yearn for beauty, experience
joy. Voluntary suffering leads to union and peace. The road of
asceticism is indeed, like love, a less traveled road but one that,
once embarked upon, offers many gracious companions and
inexplicable joys and new freedoms.[1]

*1. Asceticism is a process that makes room for God in our
lives by emptying, purging, and cleansing our minds, hearts,
and bodies.*

It is impossible to consider God as a Christian should with
heart and head full of earthly business, society, worries or
pleasures. At first it is a question of choice between good
thinking and evil, right doing and wrong; soon, however,
we realize that this is not enough; that we must also limit
the good and beautiful things to make room for God.[2]

~

In all these forms of spiritual abstinence the relative value
vanishes before the absolute one. To choose one is to
eliminate the other. Poverty itself enriches: the unclut-
tered life yields its own reward.[3]

~

First, the field of normal consciousness and conduct,
where the "I" lives in contact with the world of sense, and
under the constant stimulus of desire, must be submitted
to the purifying power; reordered in accordance with the
standards of reality. Next, the intellectual region, where
the mind is always at work analyzing and interpreting,
must subordinate the separate findings of reason to the
overwhelming certitudes of faith; and the psychic world of

1. *The Collected Works of St. John of the Cross*, trans. Kieran Kavanaugh, O.C.D.,
and Otilio Rodriguez, O.C.D. (Washington, D.C.: ICS Publications, 1973), 86.
2. Romano Guardini, *The Lord* (Chicago: Henry Regnery Company, 1954), 187.
3. Louis Dupre, *The Deeper Life: An Introduction to Christian Mysticism* (New
York: Crossroad Publishing Co., 1981), 42.

memory and imagination in which so much of our waking life is passed, must disclose its fugitive and approximate character over against God. Last, the will, the principle of action, and the very expression of our personal love and life, is to be cleansed of self-interest by the action of Divine Love that the whole unified being "reformed" in faith, hope, and charity, may tend to its one objective, the incomprehensible Being of God.[4]

St. Luke's account of the Annunciation is a marvelous example of gracious asceticism. Mary was engaged to Joseph. Plans and expectations were all in place. Suddenly God entered Mary's life with a radical request: would she be willing to forego her desires and embrace a divine plan filled with joys and sorrows, sorrows that would pierce the heart. The ultimate question here is one of inner poverty: was there room in Mary's heart for this request and all that it demanded? Her faith response gives evidence of the centrality of her relationship with God. Though she was afraid and did not understand, she proclaimed her *fiat!* Foregone were her own will, her physical intimacy with Joseph, the respect of some members within her immediate community. Such values — self-determination, physical intimacy, respect — paled, however, before the awesome mission offered to her. A disposition of openness, grounded certainly in the habit of asceticism, made possible Mary's radical response. When a new grace, the grace to bear the Redeemer, was offered, there was room within Mary for its conception and growth.

On their travels, tourists seeking accommodations watch for the "Vacancy" sign outside motels. Dismay sets in when one after the other all they see is the cruel "No Vacancy" message, which happy proprietors flip on when every room is filled. This image reflects one dimension of asceticism: occupation, or rather, preoccupation. When life is cluttered with excessive

---

4. *An Anthology of the Love of God*, from the writings of Evelyn Underhill, ed. Lumsden Barkway, D.D., and Lucy Menzies, D.D. (London: A. R. Mowbray & Co., 1976), 202.

activity, glutted with material possession, or flooded with spiritual gifts or a multitude of relationships, it can well happen that the consumption of time and energy is so great that the mystery of God is shelved, if not forgotten. There is simply no inner space left and the divine Guest remains at the door facing the blinking "No Vacancy" sign. Matters of the spirit are thus ignored or neglected. In this situation asceticism provides the function of creating space, putting us in the posture of being unoccupied. This graced vacancy speaks directly of availability.

Within life there are those rare individuals who, though laden with many duties and serious responsibilities, seem to be always accessible. Certainly, the habit of healthy asceticism resides in their being. The present moment or person is "framed" with attentiveness and concern, all else temporarily forgotten. Such a discipline is characterized by awe, wonder, and reverence. C. S. Lewis, in his autobiography, *Surprised by Joy*, shares an experience from his life's journey: "I found, as always, that the ripest are kindest to the raw and the most studious have most time to spare."[5] This style of gracious presence flowing from mortification is a tremendous grace. The psalmist states it this way: "All find a home in you" (Ps. 87:7).

2. The goal of asceticism is union with God through attentive obedience.

Asceticism here refers to those human efforts to discern and to respond in a systematic way to God's active presence in the world. The religious development which is the goal of such asceticism need not be understood as an effort at self-justification; it can be seen rather as growth in one's ability to discern patterns of God's presence within human life and to respond in an increasingly open way to this presence.[6]

~

---

5. C. S. Lewis, *Surprised by Joy* (New York: Harcourt, Brace & World, 1955), 216.

6. Evelyn Eaton Whitehead and James D. Whitehead, *Christian Life Patterns* (New York: Doubleday and Co., 1979), 36.

Outside obedience to God, mortification is not only vain, but harmful.[7]

~

This meaning of contemplation, as the knowledge of God based on the intimate and loving experience of his presence, remained the same until the end of the Middle Ages. Ascetical practices as they were developed in various forms in monastic life were always directed toward contemplation as the normal term of spiritual activity. Indeed, everything in monastic life was designed to foster and sustain this movement toward experiential union with Christ and, through him, with the Father.[8]

At the beginning of his ministry, Jesus attracted many followers by his deeds and words. Yet the gospel records that when things began to get difficult — hard sayings, conflict with authority, imposing demands — many of the initial followers walked away. Jesus, on one occasion, even asked Peter if he too would leave. Peter's famous and ironic response is imbedded in our Christian memories. Though Peter would later falter, he would also one day deny himself and allow the Lordship of Jesus to govern his life — and death. A different drummer beat in the heart of Peter: the Spirit of love and forgiveness. Here we witness a model for asceticism, someone who listened to the voice of Jesus and followed in his way. The goal of asceticism is union with the Lord; the means, that of listening and responding to his vision and values. Such attentiveness to the Lord is a contemplative posture, another dimension of asceticism.

The power of self-regard has been documented in many psychological studies. When this tendency of centering on self excludes others, life becomes distorted, resulting in significant personal and social problems. In fact, whole theories of evil are constructed around the concept of vested interest, greed,

---

7. François Roustang, S.J., *Growth in the Spirit*, trans. Kathleen Pond (New York: Sheed & Ward, 1966), 233.

8. Thomas Keating, "Contemplative Prayer in the Christian Tradition," *America* (April 8, 1978): 278.

and avarice (à la Ernest Becker). Given this reality, we need not be surprised to find that asceticism is most difficult and seldom practiced. The fulfillment of our own needs, very legitimate and necessary within boundaries, can easily become a way of life. A life of taking/receiving reduces giving to a minor virtue, if one at all. The grace of conversion is necessary if we are to break the confining circle of our egos. And underlying that conversion is obedience and contemplation. The former focuses on God's will and not our own; the latter places us in the Lord's presence where we are strengthened and healed.

The well-known story of Fr. Damien and his work with lepers captures the heart of this principle. Damien was no romantic. The pain and anguish of human life were so immediate to him that only tremendous energy and perseverance made his ministry possible, that is, the energy of grace and the perseverance of love flowing from God's redeeming presence. The constant reaching out into the lives of others, the struggle with doubts and fears, the carrying of one's own burdens and the burdens of others — how else is all this possible unless God is near and asceticism is highly developed. Though surrounded by a storm of calumny and mistrust, Fr. Damien did not capsize because his anchor of asceticism fostered union with God and obedience to the divine word.

3. Asceticism disposes a person to love and to service.

> Mortification necessarily accompanies all human relationships if they are to be loving relationships, for love always means the contradiction of our inner selfishness. . . . But in terms of penitential practices, this means that mortification can be of value only if it promotes a growth in love for Christ in his community-body.[9]

~

> This vanity and sensuality needs to be burned out of us if ever we are to love as we are loved. This is the reason

---

9. Rev. James Dallen, "Penance and the Life Situation of the Penitent" (source unknown).

for the cross: only by dying to all in ourselves that hinders love can we truly begin to live in love.[10]

~

As the tilling of the soil is necessary for its fruitfulness — untilled soil produces only weeds — mortification of the appetite is a requisite for man's spiritual fruitfulness.[11]

When Jesus washed the feet of the disciples at the Last Supper, this powerful symbolic act tells of a way of life, a life of service and love. Jesus, keenly aware of the needs of the hurting and poor, consistently reached out to them. Such a fundamental posture flowed from his sense of mission and a radical self-forgetfulness. Centering on the Father's will and desirous of bringing all peoples into union with his Father, Jesus denied himself for the sake of others and for the sake of the kingdom. The heart of Jesus overflowed with compassion and concern; his was an ascetical heart abounding in joy.

Sentinels must necessarily be capable of asceticism if they are to fulfill their role of service to the community. Their function in a given culture or society is to be on the outlook for enemies who could injure or destroy people and values. Foregoing sleep and other legitimate activities, the sentinel stands guard while others rest or tend to their personal goals. Sentinels are called to an outer and inner vigilance, a watching and waiting that is incompatible with self-indulgence. A satiated night sentinel could easily fall asleep; a distracted sentinel might easily miss the sounds of the approaching enemy; a preoccupied sentinel fails to be alert. In a sense, all of us are sentinels called upon to protect others from harm and to assist them in their needs. This is possible only if we are willing to forego many legitimate uses of our time and energy. The disposition of a caring and loving sentinel is necessary for authentic service and love.

---

10. Thomas H. Green, *When the Wells Runs Dry* (Notre Dame: Ave Maria Press, 1979), 89.

11. *The Collected Works of St. John of the Cross*, 90.

A famous Shakespearean character had a lean and hungry look, but his look did not stem from spiritual asceticism. Rather, such deprivation of body and spirit was programmed for manipulation and exploitation, for a self-getting and not a self-giving. By way of contrast, spiritual leanness puts us on edge so that we might be sensitive to the pains and needs of others. Here asceticism not only has liberation as a primary goal but also compassion. By means of spiritual asceticism we suffer with others. Their pain and agony in some way becomes ours and elicits from us an active response of concern. Though this is essentially a spiritual phenomenon we see a parallel on the physical level: less physical bulk demands less energy for self and frees us to use that energy for others. The amount of personal and collective energy is limited. Again the interdependence among the physical, psychological, social, and spiritual dimensions of the human journey becomes evident. Asceticism affects every level of our being.

4. Asceticism influences the effectiveness of prayer and is itself conditioned by prayer.

And such mortification will leave its impress upon our prayer life. One act of self-denial with the master motive of love behind it can transform our praying from the beating of the empty air into the power that removes mountains. There is only one secret of prevailing prayer — the love that crucifies self, and enthrones God in a lifelong series of definite acts of love; and when we come to analyze these acts, we shall see that behind even the most spontaneous and positive of them is the practice of daily mortification.[12]

~

We shall have overcome a considerable obstacle when prayer and penance condition each other, for their unity will be able to become the guarantee of their orientation.

12. E. Herman, *Creative Prayer* (Cincinnati: Forward Movement Publication, n.d.), 97.

If it is necessary to deprive oneself of food and sleep, it is not to establish a performance or glorify oneself over an exploit, but to allow the spirit to give itself freely to prayer, since, if it is less strongly captivated by the things of earth, it will be able to give attention to what is above it.[13]

~

We shall not fail to observe the fasts, disciplines and periods of silence which the Order commands; for as you know, if prayer is to be genuine it must be reinforced with these things — prayer cannot be accompanied by self-indulgence.[14]

In the garden of Gethsemane, Jesus' prayer life and asceticism came together in a powerful confluence. Face to face with the mystery of death, our Lord struggled to embrace the will of his Father in prayer as every cell in his body clung desperately to life. How would the crisis end? Would Jesus be able to forego his very life in response to the redemptive plan? The Gethsemane experience was not the first garden of sacrifice and denial that Jesus confronted nor was it the first long night of prayer from whence he drew strength and courage.

Eventually all of us come to the water's edge. There the fundamental option of life must be made: stand there and look at one's reflection, as did Narcissus, or plunge into the fullness of life through baptism in Christ. Prayer is that plunge into the mind and heart of God, attentive to his word and willing to participate in his mission. Entering such a relationship has many consequences: the initial coolness of a strange world; the surrender of a treasured self-determination to obedience; the exposure of our souls to a mysterious silence and haunting solitude. Prayer, that means of nurturing our relationship with the Lord, is sometimes not practiced because we dread the demands of discipleship. The ascetical side of our friendship with God makes us hesitant and afraid. Always more will be asked

---

13. Roustang, *Growth of the Spirit*, 232.
14. *The Complete Works of St. Teresa of Jesus*, ed. and trans. E. Allison Peers (London: Sheed & Ward, 1944), 2:16.

of us and we are not sure that sacrifice is the greatest path to happiness. As prayer will call us to ever deeper denial, so too a deepening asceticism enriches the quality of our prayer.

Monica, the mother of St. Augustine, was a woman of deep prayer. She interceded with God to heal her son from darkness, to save him from his sinful ways. As we known from the *Confessions*, Monica's prayer was eventually answered. *Eventually!*

One incident in Monica's life shows what happens when prayer and asceticism are divorced. Monica begged the Lord to keep her son near her in their homeland of northern Africa. Her prayer contained much selfishness and was not answered. By means of deception, Augustine sailed away in the night and eventually went to Milan, where he met Ambrose, a man of God who influenced his conversion. Had Augustine stayed in Africa according to Monica's plan, God's design would have been thwarted. Only when prayer is preceded by asceticism are we able to surrender our wills to the Lord. Monica suffered much in not living that lesson.

5. Asceticism fosters a mature freedom, a primary goal of the spiritual life.

> Paradoxically also, the pure beauty, the unbounded love, the perfect freedom which are the ends of our spiritual life seem attainable only through a measure of asceticism and self-denial, the acceptance of discipline, the adoption of a regimen.[15]

~

> And freedom cannot abide in a heart dominated by the appetites — in a slave's heart; it dwells in a liberated heart, which is a son's heart.[16]

~

> Obedience, fasting and prayer are laughed at, yet only through them lies the way to real, true freedom. I cut off

---

15. Michael F. McCauley, ed., *On the Run: Spirituality for the Seventies* (Chicago: Thomas More Association, 1974), 31.

16. *The Collected Works of St. John of the Cross*, 80.

superfluous and unnecessary desires. I subdue my proud and wanton will and chastise it with obedience, and with God's help I attain freedom of spirit and with it spiritual joy.[17]

In our Lord's passion, we see Pilate as one who lacked mature freedom even though he held an office that involved the work of justice. Enslaved by fears and swayed by public pressure, this political leader condemned Jesus without due process. Such a lack of freedom is not unique to Pilate. With life's experiences, we become increasingly aware of how unfree we are. Commitment, dedication, and loyalty, though much desired in the abstract, fail to find concrete expression because of obstacles impeding our choices. St. Paul's struggle (Romans 7) captures well the universal dilemma that befalls human nature: doing the unwanted, failing to realize desires. Freedom is both a gift and a task. The seed that is given must be nurtured, developed, and exercised through our lives. Asceticism is central to the process of authentic liberation and the maturation of freedom. Without it, we become enslaved by our own vested interests.

Students attending the Juilliard School of Music voluntarily enter a rigorous, ascetical regimen. Only after countless hours and years of determined effort does the violist, flautist, or pianist gain sufficient freedom to "create" music, not just play music. An invisible but real line is crossed here. Discipline takes us up to the threshold of freedom's house and makes entrance possible. The shackles of structure and mechanical routine are broken and the musician begins to fly. Some people question whether or not the price of excellence (of freedom) is too high, for sometimes one's very personality is sacrificed in striving to excel. The argument is worth pursuing. What is not subject to controversy, however, is the simple fact that excellence will always demand great sacrifice. Union with God is no exception. Though such union is ultimately a grace, gratuitously given,

---

17. Fyodor Dostoevsky, *The Brothers Karamazov* (New York: International Collectors Library, American Headquarters, n.d.), 291.

opening our hands and hearts to receive it calls for a letting go, calls for asceticism.

The popular movie *E.T.* presents a relationship between a young earthling and an extraterrestrial creature. Fear dominates the first steps of their encounter, but gradually warmth and affection win out. The earthling, though young of heart and lacking experience, gains sufficient freedom to allow his newfound friend to return to his distant planet. No small act of courage here. For anyone of any age to allow a friend to leave demands ascetical strength. Hopefully it is not only in movies that such acts of freedom and denial are found. All of us have to struggle between the pull of self-indulgence and courageous acts of self-denial. All of us must seek deeper and deeper levels of freedom that enable us to become life-givers. The degree of our freedom is hard to measure as is the extent of our bondage. But the call is clear: to come into possession of that freedom that characterizes the sons and daughters of God. With grace and conscious effort, with faith and asceticism, our freedom will grow into full flower.

6. Asceticism must contend with certain dangers: excessiveness, vanity, and self-righteousness.

Asceticism, or the war with the appetites, is itself an appetite.[18]

~

Then arises periodically in our life, or in that of the Christian communities, the aspiration to a contorted asceticism which seems to be the shortcut to sanctity. We think we can take the initiative towards our perfection ourselves, reducing it to the mastery of our instincts, and we feel, so far as we ourselves are concerned, that it depends primarily and essentially on our will. But to crush the impulse of our vital powers or to whittle down our strength to the point of reaching a kind of insensitivity is a caricature of

---

18. G. K. Chesterton, *St. Thomas Aquinas* (New York: Doubleday Image, n.d.), 104.

the spiritual triumph. Christ Jesus did not come to reign over what was destroyed but to order every form of life by leading it to its term. If we take this so-called shortcut, we are in danger of ending up in a pharisaical pride which is the antithesis of union with God.[19]

~

Christian asceticism is always distinguished by two guiding marks: its motive is not desire to acquire superior merit, or to achieve self-improvement, but an impulse of pure love; and it begins, not with the body, but with the spirit.[20]

In the rear of the synagogue stood the pharisee and the publican. The pharisee had fulfilled certain religious obligations of no small importance: he prayed, he gave alms, he fasted. Yet, as the Lord indicates, something was tragically wrong in all this "rightness." These excellent and mandatory religious duties were seriously tainted by a distorted motive and flowed from a heart filled with pride and self-righteousness. A blatant judgmentalism turned what could have been commendable moral behavior into sour vinegar. Jesus, while not downplaying religious practice, focused on the motives that ultimately condition our spiritual works. His concern becomes clear in his reflection on the publican: the publican's inaction was not condoned, but at least his humility provided the groundwork for conversion. He went home "justified."

To clear the high hurdles, a racer must have strong legs and sufficient speed. The spiritual race confronts its own hurdles and demands its own virtues. Perhaps the greatest obstacle frustrating asceticism's purpose is pride. The temptation is to take unto oneself any spiritual growth resulting from self-denial and to compare, often unconsciously, one's own life with that of others. Success often leads to pride, comparison to odious judgmentalism and self-righteousness. All that began well, with fairly high motives and zealous commitment, collapses in

19. Roustang, *Growth of the Spirit*, 76.
20. Herman, *Creative Prayer*, 96.

sad disarray. Our almost-won freedom becomes a new slavery, and our noble deeds become infected with a spiritual cancer. Self-righteousness alienates us from our brothers and sisters, besides isolating us in the pathological world of elitism. Pride cuts us off from God and turns our steps east of Eden into a life of rebellion. Only the strength of humility and the energy of compassion prevent us from stumbling in the race. The hurdles are high, but the graces offered are many.

In his controversial and rather strange interpretation of the life of St. Francis, Nikos Kazantzakis seems to give the lie to our principle. Kazantzakis portrays the asceticism of Francis to be excessive and extreme, to say the least. Though this portrait is more fiction than fact, an interesting point is raised that must be considered: the relationship between excessive denial and love. Francis was madly in love with God. History verifies this faith response. Since love knows few boundaries, it is not surprising to have an interpretation of Francis's life in which no price, no sacrifice is too great. Nothing was too excessive if that deed or virtue led to union with God. Love can afford to be excessive when truly authentic and when it does not flow from the heart of a pathological fanatic. Francis has fascinated generations because his extravagant love was embedded in a simple, caring, compassionate human being.

7. Asceticism is characterized by joy.

And love is pure joy. Christian mortification is not a dreary penance. Its restraints are radiant with promise and hope; its austerities are the luxuries of the heart that loves. The truly disciplined soul has all the attractiveness of one who is ruled by love.[21]

~

And for the modern reader the clue to the asceticism [of St. Francis] and all the rest can best be found in the stories of lovers when they seemed to be rather like lunatics. Tell it as a tale of one of the troubadours and the wild things

---

21. Ibid., 97.

he would do for his lady, and the whole of the modern puzzle disappears.[22]

~

Do not look for rest in any pleasure, because you were not created for pleasure; you were created for spiritual joy.[23]

Throughout the gospel narrative we see that Jesus is concerned about the well-being of others both in moments of joy and suffering. This is true at the festivity of Cana and in the distress of Calvary. Jesus' concern for the wine supply, for the well-being of a thief, for the future of his mother and beloved disciple, demonstrate a radical other-centeredness. Our Lord reconciles joy with suffering, refusing to allow one to preclude the other. Today joy has become so identified with pleasure that when things are not going well then joy seems to be impossible. However, this is to narrow down the very meaning of joy. Joy is larger than suffering and is found whenever and wherever love is active — even in the midst of the deepest suffering. No occasion, be it sickness or health, storms or sunshine, peak experiences or depression, excludes the potential for joy. Its residence lies far beyond the boundaries of physiology and psychology. Joy touches the essence of life because it is always the by-product of love. In it we find that strange and subtle phenomenon of radiance and transparency.

A major consequence of suffering is self-preoccupation. A major effect of joy is liberation and expansiveness. A severe toothache can paralyze an individual and prevent any reaching out to others. It can but it need not. There are individuals who live with constant pain, physical, mental, or spiritual, yet who transcend their own situation in loving concern for others. Asceticism lies behind such transcendence. Through intentional discipline, individuals focus on the well-being of others rather than on one's own discomfort. How frequent this happens is

22. G. K. Chesterton, *St. Francis of Assisi* (New York: Doubleday and Co., 1957), 15.

23. Thomas Merton, *Seeds of Contemplation* (New York: Dell Publishing Co., 1949), 164.

hard to say; that it happens, no one can deny. Amazing grace! Amazing joy!

Neither the life nor poetry of Emily Dickinson could be characterized as possessing the quality of extravagant joy. Yet there are moments of great lightness and expansiveness that indicate periodic ecstasy. In her life, joy and suffering were inextricably bound together. Whether her self-denial was voluntarily entered into or imposed by external forces is a matter left for biographers. One thing is certain: her business was circumference. The goal was to have a large world beyond the narrow confines of her ego. Joy comes with expansion, and Emily Dickinson had momentary experiences of this reality. The paradox lies in the means to the end. Largeness of heart and life comes, in part, from ordered energies. Asceticism fosters joy through self-denial; dissipation precludes it.

8. Asceticism for the Christian is relational: one suffers in and with Christ out of love.

It is by its motive that Christian asceticism is lifted out of the region of gloom and becomes a ministry of gladness. The Christian soul longs to endure hardness, to toil, to suffer, to deny itself to the death, not for the purpose of spiritual self-aggrandizement, but out of a consuming desire to share the labors and sufferings of Him who submitted Himself to the limitations and disciplines of a poor man's life for our sakes. It was the passion to be brought into fuller sympathy and closer union with the Man of Sorrows that made St. Teresa cry out: "Let me suffer, or not live!" No mortification can be called fully Christian which is not an authentic, irrepressible movement of love.[24]

~

Hear this, every intelligent spirit: The steed swiftest to carry you to perfection is suffering, for none shall attain

---

24. Herman, *Creative Prayer*, 96.

eternal life except he pass through great bitterness with Christ.[25]

~

Believe me, daughter: it is to those whom My Father loves most dearly that he sends the greatest trials; for love and trials go together.[26]

~

Mortification, insofar as it is truly Christian, is nothing else than "the practice of the Cross." The spirit of the Cross is the soul of true prayer; for, as we have seen, prayer is fundamentally an act of self-giving.[27]

The cost of discipleship is well known to anyone who has carefully pondered the Scriptures. Daily we must pick up our cross(es) and follow in the footsteps of Jesus. Anything less is an inauthentic Christian life, for through baptism we participate in his obedience, humility, and love. It is Christ's self-giving and his response to whatever the Father asks of him that must be our own. Thus we become co-sufferers, participating in the passion so as to share in the glory of the resurrection. Love, the motive that drove the Lord in all he did and said, undergirding his works of redemption and all acts of self-donation, shapes the heart and mind of every disciple. The Carmelite poet Jessica Powers captures in verse the meaning of asceticism in the life of those who truly are the friends and disciples of Christ:

THE SIGN OF THE CROSS

The lovers of Christ lift out their hands to
the great gift of suffering.
For how could they seek to be warmed and clothed
and delicately fed,
to wallow in praise and to drink deep draughts
of an undeserved affection,
have castle for home and a silken couch for bed,

---

25. *Meister Eckhart*, 90.
26. *The Complete Works of St. Teresa of Jesus*, 1:352.
27. Herman, *Creative Prayer*, 99.

when He the worthy went forth, wounded and hated,
and grudged of even a place to lay His head?

This is the badge of the friends of the Man of Sorrows:
the mark of the cross, faint replica of His,
become ubiquitous now; it spreads like a wild blossom
on the mountains of time and in each of the crevices.
Oh, seek that land where it grows in a rich abundance
with its thorny stem and its scent like bitter wine,
for wherever Christ walks He casts its seed
and He scatters its purple petals.
It is the flower of His marked elect, and the fruit
it bears is divine.

Choose it, my heart. It is a beautiful sign.[28]

An oxen yoke is an apt symbol for a theology of asceticism
and co-ministry. In pulling the spring plow, the oxen are linked
together in a cooperative endeavor as the soil is prepared to
receive the seed. So, too, our call to asceticism. We never enter the dying process (paschal mystery/paschal ministry) alone.
The entire Christian life is of a participatory nature. Herein
lies our joy despite constant suffering. As the psalmist states so
well: a single day in the house of the Lord is better than a thousand elsewhere. The contrary experience, days of satisfaction
and pleasure apart from God, leads to indescribable anguish.
Only in living and moving and having our being in Christ is
meaning to be found.

Contemporary psychologists would have a field day in analyzing the personality of this fourteenth-century mystic:

Then suddenly it came into my mind that I ought to wish
for the second wound as a gift and a grace from our Lord,
that my body might be filled full of recollection and feeling of the blessed Passion, as I had prayed before, for I
wished that his pains might be my pains, with compassion which would lead to longing for God. . . . I desired to

---

suffer with him, living in my mortal body, as God would give me grace.[29]

For most people there seems to be sufficient sorrow in any given day to tax the endurance and patience of the heartiest soul. Seldom would there arise the need to ask for suffering. But is this not to miss the point? People who truly love must be with the beloved in that person's joys and sorrows. Lovers refuse to be separated even when their union involves suffering and death. Christians are challenged to embrace the glory of the risen Christ but also to suffer with and in his body, the church. Asceticism, that voluntary participation in the full life of another, is essentially relational. This "practice of the cross" is a necessary element in our living the sacraments of initiation. It is to live continuously our baptism, confirmation, and eucharistic lives. No more eloquent testimony of this commitment can be given than that of St. Paul, a master and model of asceticism:

> Who will separate us from the love of Christ? Trial, or distress, or persecution, or hunger, or nakedness, or danger, or the sword? As Scripture says: "For your sake we are being slain all the day long; we are looked upon as sheep to be slaughtered." Yet in all this we are more than conquerors because of him who has loved us. For I am certain that neither death nor life, neither angels nor principalities, neither the present nor the future, nor powers, neither height nor depth nor any other creature, will be able to separate us from the love of God that comes to us in Christ Jesus, our Lord. (Rom. 8:36–39)

9. Asceticism strives to reverence every dimension of life: physical, emotional, and spiritual.

Here is the crux of the matter. We believe in physical mortification, not because we esteem the body as vile, but, on the contrary, because our faith in the Incarnation pledges

---

29. Julian of Norwich, *Showings*, trans. from the critical text with an introduction by Edmund Colledge, O.S.A., and James Walsh, S.J. (New York: Paulist Press, 1978), 180–81.

us to a high conception of the body's sanctity and destiny. Mortification is not the sacrificing of the body to the alleged interest of the soul: it is the expression of the soul's regard for the body as an instrument of holiness. The body is meant to be not the mere outer garmenting, but the palpitant medium of the soul — to take on its mold, and to glow with its splendor. It is destined itself to become spiritual, not by means of a process of inanition, as a false asceticism would have us believe, but by a gradual transfiguration in which no natural endowment is lost.[30]

~

One certain criterion of the positive orientation of our works will consist in the will to make prayer and penance coincide with them. We shall be able to oscillate for a long time between one and the other of these practices and we shall even frequently have the impression that we are leading at the same time several lives which do not fit in with each other. What we give to prayer, we shall think we are withdrawing from action, and, conversely, because of the latter, we shall regret not spending a sufficient time with God. Similarly in the abstinences of which we force ourselves, we shall be tempted to see a diminution of our living strength which could be placed at the service of others. These difficulties are normal.[31]

~

No doubt the Church felt it must throw in its lot with man's spiritual development, his sensuality already being sufficiently strong. The result, however, has not been the unification of personality, but the denial of wholeness, and a swing from one opposite to the other. So in Western history we have a continual seesawing back and forth of extremes of spiritual asceticism on the one hand, and sensuality on the other. Nor have the values of the spirit ever been realized through the repression of the senses, for

---

30. Herman, *Creative Prayer*, 104.
31. Roustang, *Growth in the Spirit*, 240.

often the spirit is reached through the senses, and sometimes spiritual development arouses and needs sensual love in order to be grounded and become substantial. In seeking to avoid the conflict of the opposites by the denial of one side of life, damage has been done to the spirit of wholeness.[32]

The rich gospel enigma that only the person who loses his/her life will save it lies at the center of a theology of asceticism. Only prayer and experience give entrance into this mystery. At first, "losing one's life" seems to negate life. Our culture tends to hold that denial is equated with rejection, deprivation with death, sacrifice with failure of spirit. A fatal dualism sets in to destroy the integrity of the personality. Body and spirit are held in opposition, each functioning in a deadening autonomy. While recognizing the disorder and darkness caused by personal and collective sin, Christian asceticism reverences the body, the emotions and the spiritual faculties as a whole. Every power and faculty, created by God, has intrinsic worth. Anything or anyone who would denigrate any aspect of creation acts in opposition to the teaching of the gospel. Always, deprivation that comes through ascetic practices must be a means to an end. We empty ourselves at every level not for the sake of emptying, but for the sake of union with God. Thus asceticism leads to peace, order, and truth.

In harvest time the vineyard rejoices with ripe fruit. Not so in the pruning season. As the vine dresser shears off all branches that would dissipate the limited energies of the vine, an ignorant observer would judge such activity as cruel and heartless. Indeed, even the vine, were it blessed with a personality, might cry out in dismay at such inhumane treatment. But the vision of the vine dresser prevails. The pruning blade causes death to those branches that impede a full harvest. Again the paradox remains: death leading to life, denial fostering fulfillment, chosen limitation leading to bounty.

---

32. John A. Sanford, *The Invisible Partners* (New York: Paulist Press, 1980), 8.

Literature provides an example of the innate tension surrounding the ascetical life. In Fyodor Dostoevsky's *The Brothers Karamozov*, a central character, Alyosha, is described in these terms: "You're a sensualist from your father, a crazy saint from your mother."[33] The novel goes on to unfold the various movements and swings between healthy enjoyment of sensual gifts and the appropriate role of self-denial. Reverence demands proper appreciation and right use of all our powers. In the novel, as in so much of life, the extremes of sensuality or unhealthy repression tend to dominate. When reverence is lacking, there is little chance that mortification will lead to life.

10. Asceticism demands that choices be made among a variety of goods and values: saying yes to one means saying no to others.

The great silent men, who judged even lawful pleasure inexpedient for Christ's athletes, and voluntarily narrowed their lives and emptied themselves of many things they would jealously have coveted had they not coveted the One Thing even more jealously — it has always been they who anticipated the world's greatest reforms, inspired it with its noblest ideals, brought loveliness out of the unlovely, and by their poverty made many rich.[34]

~

We can then realize how much easier it is to say "No" instead of "Yes" to oneself, and why all asceticism is first designed to serve this great "Yes."[35]

~

A love of pleasure and attachment to it, usually fires the will toward the enjoyment of things that give pleasure. A more intense enkindling of another better love (love of one's heavenly Bridegroom) is necessary for the vanquishing of the appetites and the denial of this pleasure. By finding his satisfaction and strength in this love, a man

33. Dostoevsky, *The Brothers Karamazov*, 70.
34. Herman, *Creative Prayer*, 30–31.
35. Johannes B. Metz, *Poverty of Spirit* (Ramsey, N.J.: Paulist Press, 1968), 8.

will have courage and constancy to deny readily all other appetites. The love of one's Spouse is not the only requisite for conquering the strength of the sensitive appetites; an enkindling with longings of love is also necessary. For the sensory appetites are moved and attracted toward sensory objects with such cravings that if the spiritual part of the soul is not fired with other more urgent longings for spiritual things, the soul will neither be able to overcome the yoke of nature nor enter the night of the senses; nor will it have the courage to live in the darkness of all things by denying its appetites for them.[36]

Jesus offers us an implicit theology of asceticism in the parable of the precious pearl. When someone finds such a valuable stone and truly treasures it, then all else is disposable. The gospel pearl that attracts the disciple is an intimate relationship with the Lord and the call to follow in his way. Once discovered, all else is relativized. A new light nuances all other possessions and goals.

However, discovery of the pearl is one thing; selling everything to obtain it is another. Many walk away from the demands of discipleship and friendship with the Lord. Their no indicates that other values supersede the gospel invitation. Those who say yes assume new responsibilities and privileges that shape their identities and destinies. All "maybes" here are unacceptable.

The hummingbird, at least from a distance, seems to be extremely greedy. In constant motion from one flower to the next, it is unable to exercise the ascetic principle of limitation. Unsatisfied or satiated by one flower, the bird is off to the next. Embedded deep within the human spirit is the drive toward "hummingbirdness" — a Faustian hunger to have all of it, abhorring any restriction or restraint. Would that we could learn at a young age the lesson of being "normal":

---

36. *The Collected Works of St. John of the Cross*, 105.

. . . the "normal" man bites off what he can chew and digest of life, and no more. In other words, men aren't built to be gods, to take in the whole world; they are built like other creatures, to take in the piece of ground in front of their noses.[37]

Asceticism demands that we construct a healthy theology of limitation (it also demands the employment of a theology of stretching). The practice of saying no to the many so that one can say yes to the master value makes commitment possible. A corollary: one root cause for lack of commitment in our society is an absence of a developed and consistent asceticism.

Modern plays depict failures and successes of asceticism. One immediately comes to mind: Robert Bolt's excellent drama *A Man for All Seasons*. Sir Thomas More, exercising a mature freedom in saying yes to his God, knew that his loyalty to King Henry, his country, and his family would be questioned. There was no doubt that More's faith relationship was primary, and because of this all other relationships were reduced to a secondary status. Adherence to this ascetical choice for Thomas More meant physical death. From another perspective, such a commitment meant eternal life. The price was willingly though painfully paid. In yet another chapter in this story we see another character named Rich, who was an opportunist without integrity. Any and every relative good attracted his fancy and his energies. For minor stones he would forgo the great pearl. Paradoxically, his desire to have all resulted in having nothing, for without asceticism no ultimate choice can be made.

The spiritual journey has a clear goal: union with God. It is through prayer, service, and asceticism that we travel this narrow road. The maps describing prayer and service are abundant; not so with asceticism. This essay attempts a brief sketch of this gospel call and notes a few markings along the way. How-

---

37. Ernest Becker, *The Denial of Death* (New York: Free Press, 1973), 178.

ever less traveled this road of asceticism may be, eventually we all come to *the* crossroad, more accurately, to the cross on the road. Whether or not we embrace that cross with Jesus depends upon the practice and habit of asceticism.

Chapter 4

PRINCIPLES OF
SPIRITUAL DIRECTION

A spiritual director on my journey once offered me a principle that I have treasured over the years: "When all is said and done; when you have tried every avenue and still have not succeeded in achieving a goal or resolving a problem, then simply say a Hail Mary and do the best you can."

That principle has served me well. Yet it does contain a note of simplicity that is somewhat unrealistic. Principles other than saying a Hail Mary and doing the best one can are also needed in making our journey toward the kingdom, principles that help point the way and challenge us to attitudes and actions that will assist in discerning and doing God's will. I decided it would be profitable to gather together some of these principles. Some are found hidden in dusty tomes in libraries, others are embedded in historical events, still others modeled by individuals who attempt to live lives of love and justice. In so doing I realize how selective I have been and that my own perception limits the range and articulation of these guidelines. Readers can supplement any deficiency by using their own experience and study.

The methodology I have selected is to state a principle, demonstrate its meaning from a variety of sources and then offer a brief commentary. Aware that principles are one step removed from experience and that experience is at the heart of our spiritual lives, we would do well to apply each principle to our own travels on the road of faith. By so doing, principles take on flesh and blood, thereby losing some portion of their innate abstractness. One thing is certain: spirituality is not concerned with abstraction. There is nothing more real and concrete than the touch of God's hand upon the human soul. Principles simply hint at what that touch is all about.

1. Spiritual direction is an interpersonal process of growth in which God's call is heard and responded to in faith.

Spiritual direction can be understood as a process, carried out in a one-to-one interpersonal context, of establishing and maintaining a growth-orientation (that is, direction) in one's faith life. This process has two moments which are in a constant dialectical relationship with each other, namely, listening to and articulating God's call in one's life, and progressively elaborating an integrated and adequate response to that call.[1]

~

It is what spiritual direction is all about. To be able to cooperate with the voice of the Spirit within us and, by obediently listening to that voice, permit the realization of God's will to take place within our lives.[2]

~

Spiritual direction: an interpersonal relationship in which one person assists others to reflect on their own experience in the light of who they are called to become in fidelity to the Gospel.[3]

1. Sandra Schneiders, I.H.M., "The Contemporary Ministry of Spiritual Direction," *Chicago Studies* (Spring 1976): 123.

2. Francis W. Vanderwall, S.J., *Spiritual Direction: An Invitation to Abundant Life* (Ramsey, N.J.: Paulist Press, 1981), 4.

3. Katherine Marie Dyckman, S.N.J.M., and L. Patrick Carroll, S.J., *Inviting the Mystic, Supporting the Prophet: An Introduction to Spiritual Direction* (Ramsey, N.J.: Paulist Press, 1981), 20.

To grow or not to grow: that is the question! Hamlet's spiritual director should have helped the distraught prince deal with growth before attempting to handle the larger question of existence, though the two questions are not unrelated. Hamlet is not alone in facing the challenges of life. Everyone of us is confronted with the growth question. Will we become the mature persons God calls us to be? Will the seeds of love, implanted in our hearts at the moment of creation, germinate and flourish on our pilgrim journey?

In spiritual direction the primary growth question lies within the area of faith. What makes matters so difficult is that faith is so inclusive, not only touching our relationship with God but also embracing every aspect of our life: the physical, personal, interpersonal, social, political, economic. God's call, heard in a faith stance, summons us to love in all our dealings. Therein is the principle of simplicity that unifies our complex lives. Though our relationships and the resulting responsibilities are numerous, yet only one thing is necessary: love. Spiritual direction is about that process of experiencing God's deep love and sharing that grace in every moment of our life.

The road to Emmaus is well worn. Its markings are many. Heavy with the problems of life, we plod our weary way looking for a companion who will help us interpret our personal scriptures, our story filled with tears and joys. Alone and without a guide we falter in our understanding and complexities. The very sound of a human voice, filled with concern and respect, is a consolation of no small worth. That voice helps us to search out the meaning of our story and achieve God's will. Edith Wharton's *Ethan Frome* presents a fascinating account of what happens to an individual when there is no companion on the road. The loneliness of despair and the absence of growth can be felt on almost every page. Spiritual direction offers a companion, not to remove our pain and struggle, but to help us to interpret all things in the light of eternity.

2. Spiritual direction attempts to foster a courageous discerning heart that seeks to discover and achieve God's will.

... the person with a converted heart is different from one with an unconverted heart. Both may engage in action for social justice, but their hearts are different. The difference in hearts is what spiritual direction is about.[4]

~

Basically, as I see it, "discernment" may be defined as the meeting point of prayer and action. That is, discernment is the art of recognizing what God is asking of us — what he would like us to do with our lives, how he wishes us to respond to the concrete life-situations which we encounter in following our vocation.[5]

~

Later on when perfection was set before me, I understood that to become a saint one had to suffer much, seek out always the most perfect thing to do, and forget self. I understood, too, there were many degrees of perfection and each soul was free to respond to the advances of the Lord, to do little or much for Him, in a word, to choose among the sacrifices He was asking.[6]

In his poem "The Road Not Taken" Robert Frost concludes that what makes all the difference in life is choosing the less traveled road. No one can deny the importance of the path chosen. Once that decision is made so much of life inexorably follows. Yet a poetic choice in contrast to an ordinary one is not of the essence. What makes the difference is the texture of one's heart. Spiritual direction focuses on whether or not our

---

4. William A. Barry and William J. Connolly, *The Practice of Spiritual Direction* (New York: Seabury Press, 1982), 197.

5. Thomas H. Green, S.J., *Darkness in the Marketplace* (Notre Dame: Ave Maria Press, 1981), 69.

6. John Clarke, O.C.D., ed. *Story of a Soul: The Autobiography of St. Therese of Lisieux* (Washington, D.C.: ICS Publications, Institute of Carmelite Studies, 1975), 27.

hearts have chosen the royal road of conversion. If so, we follow the master to Jerusalem whether at our desk, in the field, or with the poor. If not, we get lost down blind alleys. Coming to know the heart of Jesus and being transformed by the love found there is what makes the difference. Herein we find our true identity.

Spiritual direction deals with a variety of goals: the affective goal of transforming our hearts (above), the cognitive goal of thinking like Christ, the behavioral goal of living the gospel. Discernment, a gift to be prayed for daily, enables us to sense the subtle stirrings and movements of the Lord. Discernment is indeed an art, a form of spiritual sensibility, that lies more with intuition than with explicit consciousness. Hints, clues, whisperings are the inadequate words we conjure up in seeking to describe the drawings and leadings of the Spirit. Endangered by too much activity and threatened by any form of satiation, discernment is an endangered species. It must be nurtured with due reverence. Just as our physical gifts, such as seeing and hearing, can be impaired by excess or deficiency, so too our spiritual seeing and hearing can be injured by inner and outer forces. Spiritual direction seeks to monitor the exercise of the gift of discernment and to foster its development.

The last judgment scene in Matthew's Gospel (chap. 25) provides criteria in ministry of spiritual direction. The sheep are those who not only had discerning hearts but actually met the needs of others; the goats are those who failed to respond to those in want. The gift of courage is needed to supplement the heart's love and the mind's discernment. Only then is Christian maturation truly achieved. Our faith life can be abortive whenever we do not allow grace to come to full term. Simply knowing God's will and having strong loving feelings are insufficient for discipleship. Service authenticates our commitment to the Lord. Courage to die to our selfishness is a necessary grace on our faith journey. Spiritual direction will specifically focus on this testing ground of action.

3. Spiritual direction, while dealing at times with problems and crises, is primarily concerned with integrated growth in faith.

Fundamentally, the skill of the good spiritual guide consists in the ability to create and maintain a growth situation.[7]

~

A psychiatrist friend of mine says that all he can do psychologically is to help mend a few broken bones so that a person can continue his or her journey. He can get them moving, but he cannot tell them which road to take. For us to choose the direction of growth and change (especially when, on one level, the end of it all is death), there has to be faith.[8]

~

As with any growth, there were fears associated with the changes in his [Merton's] life. He might yearn for solitude but he also knew that there were dangers attached to it, that it threw a man back on his own resources in a way that aroused anxiety, depression, and many other emotions.[9]

A formula that may be of assistance in direction is what I call the DEP formula: D=disposition, E=experience, P=process. Growth happens when people are properly disposed. An uncultivated field is ill-prepared to receive and nurture the spring seed. The ground is too hard, too weedy, too stony. A good director is consistently working on the disposition of the directee, checking out the texture of the spiritual soil: open or closed, rigid or flexible, dominated by hope or discouragement. Disposition colors experience so profoundly that entire seasons of one's life can be missed because of being "out of sorts" and moody. On the underside of experience is process. What we do and what happens to us must be reflected upon

7. Schneiders, "The Contemporary Ministry of Spiritual Direction," 132.

8. Alan Jones, *Exploring Spiritual Direction: An Essay on Christian Friendship* (New York: Seabury Press, 1985), 47.

9. Monica Furlong, *Merton: A Biography* (New York: Harper & Row, 1980), 284.

and examined for meaning and implications and then appropriated. Failure to process causes such diseases as confusion, fatigue, anomie, burn-out. Growth is premised on disposition and process. A primary responsibility in spiritual direction is to evaluate what is happening in these two segments of life.

Jesus invited the rich young man to walk a different road. A problem existed in that invitation because it touched a heart preoccupied with things. There was no apparent moral problem here nor lack of desire. Rather, the many possessions of the young man became a burden rather than a gift. Jesus, as spiritual director, was dealing here with a problem, a crisis. It involved something in the area of greed and avarice; the inability of the young man to be poor in spirit. All spiritual directors must deal with similar difficulties. Yet direction is not essentially the ministry for resolving such issues. The focus is primarily on one's relationship to God. When problems surface they cannot be shunned. If properly trained the director will be of assistance. However, problems are not to become the central focus in direction.

Spiritual directors should not be surprised if resistance is commonly encountered in their ministry. Growth is not easy. It involves the unknown and that experience often overflows into fear. Of all emotions, fear will surface in direction with great frequency (to be exceeded only by anger). Direction, therefore, must revert to divine providence and trust, the nutrients for any growth of faith. Encouraging directees to have keen memories of the marvelous deeds of God is one way of dealing with fear. Experiencing God's love from these past events helps to drive out fear that can paralyze us as we move into the future.

4. Spiritual direction is effective when growth is manifest in an increase of love, fidelity, and responsible care.

Have they the *marks* of peace, love, wisdom and humility on their faces or in their conversion?[10]

---

10. Roger Lancelyn Green and Walter Hooper, *C. S. Lewis: A Biography* (New York: Harcourt, Brace, Jovanovich, 1974), 121.

~

The requirements for effective ministry in the area of spiritual direction are determined by the final end of the process itself, namely, the spiritual maturity of the directee. Spiritual maturity is a fully integrated life with God characterized by freedom, fidelity, and fruitfulness.[11]

~

He was aware of an immense load of responsibility: it was indistinguishable from love.[12]

Evaluation has become a part of our lives, be it business, teaching, administration, ministry. One reason lies in the justifiable demand of accountability: tasks are to be accomplished with competency and responsibility. Spiritual direction is not exempt from this evaluative process. How do we know whether or not this ministry is truly effective, whether or not it "works"? Several markings help us to chart this ministry: directees advancing in the quality of their love, in a persistent faithfulness to their vocation whether in the winters of discontent or in the droughts of summer, a responsible care demonstrated in service to others. When these attitudes and practices are present there is some assurance that good spiritual direction is being experienced.

St. Paul's letter to the Colossians is an excellent manual for spiritual directors. Unabashed by extravagance, Paul describes the components of Christian living. Hopefully he was referring to the entire community, since no one individual could carry the weight of these moral imperatives. His list provides evaluative criteria:

Because you are God's chosen ones, holy and beloved, clothe yourselves with heartfelt mercy, with kindness, humility, meekness, and patience. Bear with one another; forgive whatever grievances you have against one another.

---

11. Schneiders, "The Contemporary Ministry of Spiritual Direction," 130.
12. Graham Green, *The Power and the Glory* (New York: Viking Press, 1940), 90.

Forgive as the Lord has forgiven you. Over all these virtues
put on love, which binds the rest together and makes
them perfect. (3:12–14)

While emphasizing effectiveness and growth, we must in-
corporate into our reflections a paradox: our power lies in our
powerlessness. Again St. Paul gives us the key: "Therefore I am
content with weakness, with mistreatment, with distress, with
persecutions and difficulties for the sake of Christ; for when
I am powerless, it is then that I am strong" (2 Cor. 12:10)
Strange to say, there are seasons of the spiritual life when our
"ineffectiveness" (Paul's weakness) makes it possible for God's
Lordship to be more manifest. This is not to endorse apathy
over love, infidelity over faithfulness, irresponsibility over care.
Yet in moments of failure and even sin, grace can reach deeper
levels of our being and bring about a more substantive conversion. Explanations here falter. Experience, however, verifies
the reality. Note must be taken of this strange phenomenon lest
we leave the land of mystery and move into a "management by
objective" mentality. The sanctuary has its own unique set of
rules that go beyond other disciplines and paradigms.

*5. Spiritual direction is concerned with disposition,
experience, and process, three factors conditioning the
quality of life.*

It is worthy of note that God does not place His grace and
love in the soul except according to its desire and love.[13]

~

Each step in one's spiritual development is the result of
definite experiences.[14]

~

13. *The Complete Works of St. John of the Cross*, trans. Kieran Kavanaugh, O.C.D.,
and Otilio Rodriguez, O.C.D. (Washington, D.C.: ICS Publications, Institute of
Carmelites Studies, 1973), 462.
14. Arthur Koestler, *Darkness at Noon* (New York: Macmillan Co., 1941), 69.

What we call the beginning is often the end
And to make an end is to make a beginning.
The end is where we start from.[15]

The DEP formula, mentioned earlier, needs a more extensive commentary. Quality of life is an expression with many connotations. Essentially we contrast it with a style of life that is superficial, subhuman, lacking in purpose. Quality implies depth, a rich humanness, meaning. Spiritual directors must be concerned with quality of life at every level. Three factors promote quality: proper disposition, appropriation of experience, consistent processing of life's experiences.

Disposition. The reason why the horse led to water did not drink was that it lacked proper disposition: the horse simply wasn't thirsty. People who lack desire and proper motivation do not grow. Causes abound: poor self-image, a history of rejection, lack of models, fear of the unknown, emotional or intellectual underdevelopment, an absence of relational skills. Spiritual directors must constantly test the soil to find out its temperature, its texture, its degree of thirst and hunger. In one sense, a director is a "disposer," one who creates a climate in which growth can take place. Affirmation, confrontation, encouragement are some of the techniques that foster proper disposition. It is well to remember that rain in the desert often causes flash flooding. The desert floor is so baked by the sun that no moisture can penetrate. Many lessons here for spiritual direction.

Experience. Thomas Hardy's reflection is all too vivid: "Through want of it [destiny] she sang without being merry, possessed without enjoying, outshone without triumphing. Her loneliness deepened her desire."[16] Much of life is not experienced because appropriation is inhibited. Several factors may be involved: hurriedness, preoccupation, fear, a vast egoism. People in a hurry don't taste their food, see sunsets, relish

---

15. T. S. Eliot, "Four Quartets," V, lines 16–19.
16. Thomas Hardy, *The Return of the Native* (New York: New American Library, 1959), 79.

a poem. People that speed through life may lap up the miles but they seldom see the flowers or experience the Lord's comings. Preoccupation means that though we are in a certain spatial zone, we are not really present. Experiences are missed; life passes us by. Fear too can so dominate our consciousness and emotional space that love cannot get through. Ultimately it all comes down to a type of self-centeredness that imprisons us in our own little egos, letting no sunshine in nor giftedness out. Spiritual directors will be attuned to these obstacles that prevent us from tasting life to the full.

Process. Before moving from lunch to dinner a process of assimilation takes place. Unfortunately this processing time is not always provided for at the emotional and spiritual level. It is possible to lunch on fear or brunch on some grace and quickly move to a dinner menu without "processing" that fear or grace. Unprocessed experiences, even very good ones, tend to dehumanize. Spiritual direction is an explicit time of processing. What happens here models a pattern that should characterize the entire journey.

6. Spiritual direction should provide an atmosphere of unconditional love; this environment models the very climate of prayer.

... only the presence of love enables us to see an object truly.[17]

~

All love, all pity and tenderness, enlarges, warms and refines the heart.[18]

~

What is involved in an atmosphere? If we were fish, our atmosphere would be water. As land animals, our atmosphere is air. In this sense, an atmosphere is that in which a species lives and moves and has its being. The atmosphere

17. Romano Guardini, *The Life of Faith*, trans. John Chapin (Westminster, Md.: Newman Press, 1961), 63.
18. Maisie Ward, ed., *The Letters of Caryll Houselander: Her Spiritual Legacy* (New York: Sheed & Ward, 1965), 62.

provides the background as well as the main ingredients, the possibilities and the limitations of a species' life.[19]

Spiritual direction is a privileged moment and ministry. Beyond the skills of the director and the good will of the directee something extremely profound is operative when two people come together to reflect on a person's faith journey. That something is grace: God's presence and love freely given. Another way of expressing this is by talking of atmosphere, climate, milieu. Created by God's Spirit, this graced moment is also conditioned by the personalities of the people who sit and talk face to face. Ideally the atmosphere will reflect the mystery of God: unconditional Love.

Shakespeare speaks of kindness in a rather dark world:

> That light we see burning in my hall.
> How far that little candle throws his beams!
> So shines a good deed in a naughty world.[20]

Given the troubled journey of so many of us pilgrims, direction should be a special oasis that is nonthreatening, affirming, and offers the experience of peace. The spiritual director has a special responsibility in this regard: to be an instrument of God's tender love and mercies. Because of the vicissitudes of life, this responsibility is difficult to realize in certain seasons. Anxious about one's own concerns, weary from heavy scheduling, simply being out of sorts, these are times in which one does not feel or even want to assume again the task of creating that unconditional space for another. Nobility is demanded here — and much grace.

Spiritual direction centers on our relationship with God. More specifically, it deals with the quality of communication in that relationship. The word is prayer! Prayer is as much an atmosphere as it is a verbal exchange. Prayer is a type of presence in which one feels encountered and changed. Modeling

---

19. Ira Progoff, *The Symbolic and the Real* (New York: McGraw-Hill, 1963), 11–12.

20. William Shakespeare, *The Merchant of Venice*, Act V, scene i, lines 88–90.

is needed in all areas of life, including prayer. A good spiritual direction session fulfills the need for example: an atmosphere of real presence, a listening and responding that is reverent, silences that are pregnant with meaning, acceptance that is healing, love that enlarges the heart. In the privacy of their own lives, both the director and directee should be able to reflect back on their sessions together to know a little more of what is to take place in prayer, that holy time and space where the Lord comes to manifest divine love and forgiveness.

7. *Spiritual direction is primarily the work of the Spirit and the director must learn to facilitate and not obstruct the action of grace.*

It is the function of therapists to help patients solve problems. But although spiritual directors may also be called upon to help solve various problems (such as blocks to prayer or obstacles to realization) their most fundamental role is to attend to God's power, love, and grace in the directee's situation. Thus, while psychological knowledge can be very helpful for spiritual directors, the thing that really counts is the director's graced capacity to intend and attend towards God.[21]

~

These directors [who do not understand souls that tread the path of quiet and solitary contemplation] do not know what spirit is. They do great injury to God and show disrespect toward Him by intruding with a rough hand where He is working. It costs God a great deal to bring these souls to this stage, and He highly values His work of having introduced them into this solitude and emptiness regarding their faculties and activity so that He might speak to their heart, which is what He always desires.[22]

~

---

21. Gerald G. May, M.D., *Care of Mind, Care of Spirit: Psychiatric Dimensions of Spiritual Direction* (New York: Harper & Row, 1982), 48.
22. *The Complete Works of St. John of the Cross*, 631.

Books are for the scholar's idle times. When he can read God directly, the hour is too precious to be wasted in other men's transcripts of their reading.[23]

The perennial debate regarding the relationship between nature and grace cannot be dismissed if only because of its long history. In spiritual direction that debate must be dealt with: what is the working of grace and how does it relate to the "natural" person? The workings of both divine and human energies must be carefully attended to, especially in a ministry that is characterized by surprises and uncertainties. One thing is clear: God is always the director. The "spiritual director" is basically a facilitator and is well advised to stay out of the way.

To forget one's proper role leads to major problems. If a director seeks too much control or forgets that God is in charge, the faith journey for the directee can be seriously jeopardized. Directors, albeit unconsciously, can begin to impose their prayer style, project their own distortions, frustrate authentic spiritual freedom, intrude on privacy. As directees reach more advanced stages of prayer there is the real possibility that the director is "left behind." This can be threatening. Further, as God exerts a more active role in the directee's life, a director must deal with a loss of power. All of this simply confirms the fact that no ministry is without some dangers.

Jeremiah the prophet spoke about the days when God would work directly with his people: "No longer will they have need to teach their friends and kinsmen how to know the Lord. All, from least to greatest, shall know me, says the Lord, for I will forgive their evildoing and remember their sins no more" (Jer. 31:34). Two things have to be protected here: God's working through the community and through specific individuals, and God's direct activity upon the human heart. At times no

---

23. Ralph Waldo Emerson, "American Scholar," *The Selected Writings of Ralph Waldo Emerson*, ed., with a biographical introduction by Brooks Atkinson (New York: Random House, 1940), 50.

intermediary will be necessary. A whole segment of spiritual literature deals with this phenomenon. Yet we know that God uses directors as instruments, making tangible and incarnate the healing power of divine love and forgiveness. To say that God works directly in human life is not to deny the sacramental principle. It merely says that God is not limited to that principle or any other. God's ways are not ours, God's thoughts are not our thoughts. These words should be etched on the walls of every spiritual director's office — better yet, on every spiritual director's heart.

8. Spiritual direction stimulates faith development when there is some accountability, specificity, and realistic expectations.

Yet, instead of blaming herself for the issue she laid the fault upon the shoulders of some indistinct, colossal Prince of the World, who had framed her situation and ruled her lot.[24]

~

Fill in the details. Fill in enough details, and the right details, and the true person will emerge.[25]

~

To expect too much is to have a sentimental view of life and this is a softness that ends in bitterness. Charity is hard and endures.[26]

Our journey of faith is extremely dynamic and developmental. Like any growing organism, our faith life is deeply influenced by "specificity." While recognizing the incomprehensibility of grace and the deep mystery of God's life within, our faith lives are very concrete and definite. In direction there has to be specificity regarding prayer, asceticism, and ser-

---

24. Thomas Hardy, *The Return of the Native*, 298.

25. Michael Mott, *The Seven Mountains of Thomas Merton* (Boston: Houghton Mifflin Co., 1984), 71.

26. Flannery O'Connor: *The Habit of Being*, letters edited and with an introduction by Sally Fitzgerald (New York: Straus and Giroux, 1979), 308.

vice. How much time and energy are given to each of these areas? What types of needs have surfaced that I am called to address? Where in my life am I not free and need to seek liberation through mortification? Development happens when we get down to time lines, allocate our limited energy in reasonable ways, make decisions in light of inner movements. Detail is at the heart of our spiritual lives; spiritual directors will necessarily be concerned about specificity.

Yet specificity serves little purpose if there is no accountability. When direction is too non-directive and is plagued with weak specification, the directee will have nothing substantive to be accountable for. On the other hand, if agendas are too rigid and specificity too exact, direction becomes a burden and can easily become a tyranny of "shoulds." Balance is needed here as in all areas of life. What can be helpful is to have some written statements (goals, contracts) that delineate in very clear terms what is hoped for in faith development. Objection to too much structure need not be taken seriously. It is better, especially in initial stages of direction, to err on the side of overstatement than to yield to nebulosity. Accountability simply means that we take our stewardship seriously. When the Master comes — or the spiritual director shows up unexpectedly — we will be found watching and waiting.

Incrementalism is a principle that we must integrate into spiritual direction. Biting off more than we can chew causes indigestion. Spiritually we should establish moderate goals and set up realistic expectations. Starting with fifteen minutes of daily prayer rather than an hour and a half makes sense; cutting down on desserts rather than skipping lunch is a beginning toward a life of fasting; offering an hour of service a week to the elderly rather than Wednesday and Friday afternoons may be more feasible. Our spirituality begins in inches and seconds. Achievable goals keep us in the land of reality and grounded on planet earth.

9. Spiritual direction, though interpersonal, contains a highly communal and ecclesial dimension.

The perfect achievement of our spiritual life is dependent on the spiritual life of every other human being.[27]

~

Community is the place where we lay ourselves open to genuine conversion. It is the corporate environment that preserves and nurtures the ongoing process of conversion.[28]

~

For the Christian, the spiritual life is faith-life, the relationship of the person with God in Christ through the power of the Spirit within the believing community.[29]

A fundamental lesson in life, hopefully learned at a relatively early age, is always to put things in context. The tendency to oversimplify and choose extremes is common. As Lisa Sowle Cahill writes: "Human beings have a preference for thinking in extremes; it makes matters far more simple. But simplicity in human affairs is more often than not illusory."[30] All of life is interrelated and cannot be properly understood without situating individual experiences in a broader perspective. Spiritual direction is no exception to this principle. This ministry relates to the whole church. Spiritual direction, though highly focused and personal, ties in with the wider life of the faith community and must be experienced and evaluated from that perspective.

From the limbs of a sycamore tree, Zacchaeus encountered Jesus. The story is familiar regarding the "hurry down," the murmuring of the crowd, the promise to assist the poor. What sometimes goes unnoticed is the fact that Jesus tells Zacchaeus that "salvation has come to your house this day." Not only was

---

27. François Roustang, S.J., *Growth in the Spirit*, trans. Kathleen Pond (New York: Sheed & Ward, 1963), 171.

28. Jim Wallis, *The Call to Conversion: Recovering the Gospel for These Times* (New York: Harper & Row, 1981), 115.

29. Schneiders, "The Contemporary Ministry of Spiritual Direction," 120.

30. Lisa Sowle Cahill, *Between the Sexes: Foundations for a Christian Ethics of Sexuality* (Philadelphia: Fortress Press, and New York: Paulist Press, 1985), 3.

this tax collector influenced by this spiritual direction session but his whole household. Our personal lives cannot be affected without simultaneously impacting all those people who are part of our lives. Through this single individual perched in a tree, many people were eventually graced. Through the faith response of one person, salvation came to many. In speaking of the ecclesial nature of spiritual direction, we necessarily include the rich tradition out of which this ministry proceeds. Directors carry into each session an accumulated wisdom of incredible proportions. The writings of the Fathers, the classical works of Teresa of Avila and Catherine of Siena (doctors of the church), the rich social encyclicals of the 1960s, the sixteen documents of Vatican Council II. The directees bring in years of faith experienced in various communities. All of this comes together and eventually returns to the community, shaping it anew and enriching it because of new and deeper commitments. Every so often it might be well for people in direction to call explicitly to mind the communal dimension of direction. Such awareness will result in gratitude and appreciation.

10. Spiritual direction is optometric in fostering a vision that is global and eschatological, immanent and transcendent.

We lose our ability to see angels as we grow older, and that is a tragic loss.[31]

~

No prophet ever sees things under the aspect of eternity. It is always partisan theology, always for the moment, always for the concrete community, satisfied to see only a piece of it all and to speak out of that at the risk of contradicting the rest of it. Empires prefer systematic theologians who see it all, who understand both sides, and who regard polemics as unworthy of God and divisive of the public good.[32]

---

31. Madeleine L'Engle, *Walking on Water: Reflections on Faith and Art* (Wheaton, Ill.: Harold Shaw Publishers, 1980), 18.
32. Walter Brueggemann, *The Prophetic Imagination* (Philadelphia: Fortress Press, 1978), 24–25.

~

What is intended here is in one respect a renewal of the
religious imagination. But it is also a particular vision of
the human lot. Nor is it only a question of elevation of
view or transcendence as in the older phrase about seeing the world in the light of eternity. It is a question rather
of heightened sensitivity for which the ordinary trans-
actions of life are shot through with meaning, with moving
charities, and with providence.[33]

A spiritual director is a kind of optometrist. A central task
is to help individuals perceive the reality of God in their lives.
Though there are many obstacles ranging from extreme myopia
to diffused far-sightedness, every effort must be made to enable
people to discern the visitations of God. Tragic is the loss of
not being able to see angels on the journey. The poet Jessica
Powers offers sage advice:

> Never go anywhere without the angels
> who watch God's face and listen to be sought.
> Greater than you, yet they have joy to serve you.
> Never go blundering through the jungle, thought,
> without a clear-eyed one to part the branches,
> shout snake or swamp-hole, cry a rock beware.
> The angels of the Lord will camp around you
> in any place you pitch your tents of prayer.
>
> Know that your soul takes radiance from the angels.
> She glories in these creatures of her kind
> and sees herself thus lightsome, free as wind.
> She stands abashed when the flesh rudely brings
> its homage to these pure intelligences
> and tries to crowd their beauty into bodies
> and weight their grace with gravity of wings.[34]

---

33. Amos Niven Wilder, *Theopoetic: Theology and the Religious Imagination*
(Philadelphia: Fortress Press, 1976), 106.
34. *Selected Poetry of Jessica Powers,* ed. Regina Siegfried and Robert Morneau
(Kansas City: Sheed and Ward, 1989, 70.

Our vision must not be limited to the range of our physical eyes and ears. Our imaginations must be trained to apprehend the workings of grace in the budding of a daisy, the host held high, the cup of cold water offered, the rising of the morning sun.

The haunting photography of the earth rise is more than just an interesting space shot. Its story, pondered and unpacked, tells of a type of human solidarity that demands a global spirituality. As the eucharistic prayer proclaims, all life, all holiness come from God. Our faith vision assists us in comprehending how God is both in time and beyond the temporal, how God is present in the smallest work of creation and is the one who transcends all creation. The ability to adjust our glasses and see from different perspectives is to be developed in spiritual direction. Direction fosters a vision that in turn molds our hearts and hands.

Milton's "Ode to Blindness" was not in praise of darkness. The poet longed to see. Yet a deeper vision is available that transcends the physical. It is the vision of faith, a vision that paradoxically embraces the midnight. By means of spiritual direction we carefully examine how God offers us a divine vision that allows us to see life as it really is. Such a ministry is a privilege and a challenge. Such a ministry instills hope in those who are lost and joy in those who discern the divine presence.

PART TWO

The Practice of
Spirituality

Chapter 5

REVERENCE

Reverence is a power, a grace, and a responsibility. Without reverence, ministry becomes manipulative, Eucharist superficial, and prayer hollow. If the Western world is marked by a growing decline of reverence, the Christian task is clear.

Several years ago when Aleksandr Solzhenitsyn gave the commencement address at Harvard University, he made the following statement, which has given me cause to ponder: "A decline in courage may be the most striking feature that an outside observer notices in the West today." If that is true, it is well worth asking what an inside observer sees. I propose that a decline in reverence characterizes the contemporary Western world. Where are the people who have the inner disposition that recognizes and responds to the sacredness of life? At every level, physical, psychological, personal, social, spiritual, life has become extremely cheap.

Tracing the footprints toward the demise of reverence would take us down some very dark paths. Yet it might be well to note some of its significant causes:

Speed: that hurriedness which brings a type of violence into relationships and experiences.

Volume: the sheer multiplicity of events that makes us insensitive, that breaks off the antennae of our hearts, minds, and senses.

Superficiality: the inability or unwillingness to live at a depth that brings with it a certain amount of suffering and pain.

Fear: constant apprehension and anxiety about possible tragedy.

Enculturation: being sucked into certain value systems and lifestyles that are foreign to human growth.

Each of these forces has a history of its own. Each has left behind a wake of devastation. And each of us needs but look within to realize the power of these forces in our own lives.

What has been lost need not remain lost. We need to seek out and find those dispositions and attitudes that will redirect our lives along paths that are life-giving. This is true of both individuals and nations.

Reverence is one of those dispositions and attitudes urgently needed today. This is not a pietistic, personal virtue; it is a profoundly communal virtue that creates an atmosphere that is conducive to growth. When political, social, economic, and cultural decisions are made in the climate of reverence, the dignity of every individual is safeguarded. When this virtue is absent, crassness and insensitivity exert their destructive force.

Areas for Reverence

The lyrics of an old song contain both good psychology and theology: "Little things mean a lot." Reverence begins with small matters or it never begins at all. A spirituality of inches and seconds is an excellent starting point for a life of reverence.

The basic challenge is to esteem the sacredness of time, knowing that each second and each hour has a certain value. Paul Tillich said it well: "The infinite significance of every moment of time is this: in it we decide, and are decided about, with respect to our eternal future."[1]

---

1. Paul Tillich, *The Shaking of the Foundations* (New York: Charles Scribner's Sons, 1948), 37.

Reverence also gives us an appreciation for the inches of our lives, that sense of sacredness of space. Step by step we work and walk toward our destiny. The propensity to disregard the small details of life leaves us poorly prepared to experience well those events that have outstanding meaning. Reverence is learned in quiet and humble moments and thus makes possible a life of quality.

Though, as an inner sensitive grace, reverence challenges us to appreciate all of time, there are special moments that demand explicit reverencing: birth, death, pain, love, victory, despair, hope — all these points in time need special recognition and reflection. If not, they will too soon be forgotten or we may well lose the connectedness and continuity of our lives. Both for a sense of identity and history, reverence is necessary. This quality fills our celebrations and anniversaries with a sacredness that doubles our joys, halves our sorrows.

Space, too, calls for the virtue of reverence. While holding all ground holy, some geographic territories, both external and internal, suggest that we remove our sandals. It is in such places that our hearts have been shaped and our relationships changed. A certain summer lake, a special room within a home, the interior castle of our soul, an autumn woods of rainbow colors, a pond where one learned to swim, a quiet church in which one's whole family celebrated life and death, a mountain peak revealing vast horizons, a grave site with its memorial stone, we come to reverence these places. They reveal encounters with God and with those we love. Spiritual delicacy for time and space is no small grace.

Motto for Reverence

The Latin expression *Ne quid nimis* loosely translated means, "Nothing whatsoever in excess." As a principle in life it contains much wisdom. Unfortunately, greed and avarice blind us to the truth of this expression and the consequences for physical health and spiritual well-being are significant.

Reverence shuns greed and avarice. It recognizes that having too much is just as dehumanizing as deprivation. Ideally the reverent person takes only as much as is needed — as much food, as much praise, as much knowledge, as much power. A basic principle underlying reverence is that it is not how much we have or how many friends we acquire but that what we have is tasted to the full and appreciated.

In a society that promotes overconsumption and consumerism it is not surprising that reverence can so easily be lost. The cultural air we breathe is not conducive to living on little. There is a demonic sense that deceives us by suggesting that the more we have the greater we are as persons. Nothing could be farther from the truth.

The fascinating hummingbird with its delicate beauty and daring aerodynamics catches our fancy. Yet, with its constant darting from blossom to blossom, the hummingbird can also make us nervous. Does the hummingbird lack reverence in its rapid and frantic flight from one flower to another? The humble bee, with its patient staying power, remains with a single flower until the nectar has all been extracted.

Our nervousness with the hummingbird perhaps tells us that the bee is a more fitting model for the human community. The point is clear, I hope: too often we are like the hummingbird in our rapid movement from one thing to another, be it a flower, a person, a word, an event. We do not reverently abide with a Mozart concerto, a Dickinson poem, a Shakespearean sonnet, a call from a friend, a paragraph of a love letter. The hummingbird syndrome makes us short circuit too much of life. Perhaps the humble bee can teach us a lesson in reverence.

Cornerstones of Reverence

In his poem "God's Grandeur," Gerard Manley Hopkins describes the brokenness and bentness of our world. Yet, despite the smears and scars, he proclaims: "there lives the dearest freshness deep down things." This sense of freshness and possibility in life is at the very core of reverence.

The ability to cut through the outer appearance and to perceive and feel intuitively the inner sacredness and dignity of life is the gift of the reverent person. This is no easy task. What is closest to us, our woundedness, often makes us blind to the beauty both within ourselves and others. A risk is here demanded, the risk of plunging into the mystery of life, into the "deep down things," and there find a hidden beauty.

This implies that hope is the twin of reverence. Hope, the virtue of the "not-yet," provides us with the capacity to dream dreams, to see what is yet to be, to encourage a gift that has not yet bloomed. Reverence for the "not-yet" contains a rich pragmatic quality, i.e., hope creates energy. As Walter Brueggemann writes: "Energizing is closely linked to hope. We are energized not by that which we already possess but by that which is promised and about to be given."[2] Reverence is not limited to what is, though it needs to appreciate present reality. Reverence looks to what may be and, because of hope, does so with a joyous enthusiasm. Like a magnetic field, reverence begins to gather around it a galaxy of other virtues, in particular enthusiasm and hope.

People who plant trees and tend flowers witness to possibility and freshness in life. Most of them have a degree of reverence running through their blood. People who nurture people and share in their pain are beyond doubt reverent creatures. Even in highly distasteful circumstances, in sickness, tragedy, and violence, there are always individuals who come and offer fresh alternatives. In *The Hiding Place*, Corrie ten Bloom speaks about people in the concentration camps who would plant flowers, a sign and moment of humanity in the midst of overwhelming evil. We all know of individuals who, in spite of terminal illness, begin a project which will be impossible to complete. Reverence for life is so deep that no brutality, not even death itself, is able to stifle all of life's potential. Reverence is what makes us human.

---

2. Walter Brueggemann, *The Prophetic Imagination* (Philadelphia: Fortress Press, 1978), 23.

Foe of Reverence

Love is the opposite of hatred. The opposite of reverence is crassness or insensitivity. But this does not say enough. What kills reverence is a deep psychological posture of futility or meaninglessness. A feeling that life is absurd militates against that stance of sacredness which helps one to find meaning in existence. Purpose is lost; the "why" cannot be answered; reverence finds no footing in this futile quagmire.

With the loss of reverence comes the sense of having wasted life. Arthur Miller captures this experience in the *Death of a Salesman:*

> And whenever spring comes to where I am, I suddenly get the feeling, my God, I'm not gettin' anywhere! What the hell am I doing, playing around with horses, twenty-eight dollars a week! I'm thirty-four years old, I oughta be makin' my future. That's when I come running home. And now, I get here, and I don't know what to do with myself. After a pause: I've always made a point of not wasting my life, and everytime I come back here I know that all I've done is to waste my life.[3]

Reverence is a matter of the heart as much as it is an attitude and call to action. A common malady infecting reverence is melancholia, the experience that something is missing in a person's life. One effect of such a dark moment is carelessness that eases into lack of respect, deadly inertia, a haunting weariness. In such an environment reverence cannot survive.

By contrast, when the sadness is countered with trust, enthusiasm, and buoyancy, then reverence thrives and becomes contagious. All this is to highlight the social dimension of the virtue of reverence. Each of us affects others by our possession or non-possession of this life quality. When it is present, we create a climate of hope and joy; when absent, that of doom and heaviness.

---

3. Arthur Miller, *Death of a Salesman* (New York: Viking Press, 1949), 22–23.

Futility and melancholia give birth to an existential angst expressed not only in cinema and fiction, but witnessed in everyday life. Christian faith offers another option and atmosphere. Faith maintains that nothing is lost, that the least and apparently most insignificant action can have eternal value. Faith is not deceived by the transitoriness of life in which everything seems to fade and then is gone with the wind. Reverence demands a belief system that can support it through storm and turmoil.

Reverence also must be incarnated in people to become credible. A keen eye can discern special moments of reverence that evidence a deep belief in life: the quality handwritten letter, the poem carefully sketched though perhaps no one will ever see it, the sacrifice of a human love for the call to service, the simple, kind word spoken to the retarded child, the visit to a grave site on a cold December day. People who have yielded to futility and melancholia do not do such things.

Offspring of Reverence

Eventually the reality of suffering and death touches everyone's life. Our reaction to these inevitable human experiences says much about who we are and whether or not reverence has found a home in our hearts. Nobility will be the touchstone of reverence at this point, for nobility is that quality within an individual or nation that refuses to respond negatively and destructively to experiences of trial and hardship.

Nobility is the offspring of reverence, the noble person embraces and accepts suffering and death as a part of human existence. Bitterness, resentment, and rage find free expression where nobility and reverence are absent.

In *I Heard the Owl Call My Name*, Margaret Craven describes with gentle sensitivity the life of an Indian tribe in western Canada. The reader recognizes a deep sense of reverence in the Indians' gracious acceptance and joy at the ebb and flow of life. Suffering and pain are embraced as are the joy-filled moments of life. The quality of nobility is present; absent, a sense of antagonism for the way life is.

Some might interpret this as a simple stoicism. That may be true except for the subtle smiles and the light and laughter in the eyes. These human graces reveal that at bottom existence has a playfulness that allows for a joyous reverence. Even when the owl calls the name of the young priest, a call that foretells his coming death, nobility perdures because of the virtue of reverence.

Teresa of Avila provides us with a piece of wisdom: "Do you think, even though it may seem so to you, that anyone has acquired a virtue when he has not tested it by its corresponding vice."[4] Reverence is not exempt from the temptations of life. Defeat and failure provide the test whether or not reverence has been internalized. If, in the face of scorn and ridicule, we respond with graciousness and kindness, then the nobility begotten by reverence manifests a high level of human and Christian maturity.

Given our weakness and sinfulness, at times we will fail. What is of paramount importance is that we quickly rise and strive with renewed effort to respond in a more loving, caring way.

A Power and a Grace

In our society there is much concern over the question of power and who possesses it. The shakers and the movers are admired because they shape many of our institutions and their policies. Seldom does the notion of reverence come up in discussions of power. And yet, the deepest changes in both individuals and systems happen when reverence is operative.

Power, the ability to bring about or prevent change, has many countenances. Often thought of in terms of specific acts and decisions, power is even more present when it creates an atmosphere or environment. It is precisely here that reverence has tremendous power, for reverence creates a spiritual climate

---

4. *The Complete Works of St. Teresa of Jesus*, ed. and trans. E. Allison Peers (London: Sheed & Ward, 1944), 1:296.

that fosters and nourishes the fullness of life. No greater power exists.

To speak of reverence is to speak of grace. It is an expression and revelation of God's presence and love in history. In a broad sense, reverence is a type of universal sacrament or sign of God's care and love. This grace quickly becomes a task, for once it is received we have the obligation to nurture it and share it with others. Reverence becomes the vocation of life.

Chapter 6

SPIRITUAL EXERCISES FOR ECLECTIC NOMADS

Health demands exercise. This is true not only of the body but also of our emotional life, our personal relationships, our spiritual endeavors. Without exercise, tonality is lost, muscles atrophy, friendships weaken, and spiritual energies diminish. Throughout the Christian tradition there have been voices urging us to foster health through exercise. St. Ignatius of Loyola was one:

> By the term "Spiritual Exercises" is meant every method of examination of conscience, of meditation, of contemplation, of vocal and mental prayer, and of other spiritual activities that will be mentioned later. For just as taking a walk, journeying on foot, and running are bodily exercises, so we call Spiritual Exercises every way of preparing and disposing the soul to rid itself of all inordinate attachments, and, after their removal, of seeking and finding the will of God in the disposition of our life for the salvation of our soul.[1]

The lesson is simple and clear: no exercise, no health.

What are some of the spiritual powers that call for attention and appropriate exercise? As starters: our capacity for intuition

---

1. *The Spiritual Exercises of St. Ignatius*, trans. Louis J. Puhl, S.J. (Chicago: Loyola University Press, 1951), 1.

and insight, the ability to reason and believe, the dynamic potentials of the heart and affections, the ranging energies of memory and recall, the creative possibilities of imagination and fantasy. As a nomad among nomads and as one who has never been able to find a taxative philosophy, psychology, or theology (thus rendering me terribly eclectic), I offer as a fellow pilgrim some of the exercises that have nourished my journey. The examples are hardly exhaustive, and I will mention other possibilities at the end of this essay. Currently, these exercises find a place in my heart: star-gazing, willow-watching, belly-laughing, story-telling, and basket-weaving. If you meet somebody on the road who is engaged in such activities, know that you are in the presence of an eclectic nomad.

Star-gazing: An Exercise in Searching

Standing in a winter field with eyes cast to the heavens is an activity that may well lead to a series of deep questions. Thousands of stars fill the galaxies and the finite human mind is overwhelmed by space and wonder of those "fire-folks" in the sky. By nature we are searchers, and a star-filled night activates our wonder, and hopefully our awe. As our eyes sweep the heavens, parts are seen in the context of the whole, narrow parochialism gives way to an ecumenical heart, courage surges through our bloodstream, enabling us to dream impossible dreams.

Stars indeed are mighty good companions, for they teach us lessons and instruct us in their lofty wisdom. First of all they tell of the creative hand of God. So vast and varied are the stars and their humble abode, the galaxies, that the human mind falters before the incomprehensibility of such beauty and space. Ursa Major hints that things are often upside down; Canis Major narrates that dogs have often been faithful human companions; Sirius reveals that some stars are brighter than others.

Analogously, we humans imitate aspects of our heavenly counterparts. St. Francis and his constellations of brothers give us a different perspective on possessions — they turn everything upside down; Dante and his assorted travelers in the

Divine Comedy reflect upon such questions as fidelity and truth; Mother Teresa and her community of caring pilgrims radiate a brilliance of glory that blinds the contemporary eye. Star-gazing, whether the stars be millions of light eyes away or right in front of our eyes, is a spiritual exercise that nurtures both faith and reason.

With sound roofs over our head, with the glare of city lights dulling the heavens, with our noses buried too deeply in the necessities of life, there is a danger that the stars will lose their power in calling us to a sense of transcendence, to the mystery of immensity. Demands for security can make us creatures of comfort; neon signs can tire our already weary eyes; the nitty-gritty of daily existence can consume our limited time and prevent habitual night walks. Star-gazing need not happen; faith and reason can atrophy or remain underdeveloped. Though no confidence is given to horoscopes or astrology, our spiritual health can be enriched by watching the stars and being attuned to their wisdom.

Willow-watching: An Exercise in Discernment

A friend once described to me her experience of watching a weeping willow. The tree stood in a courtyard with drooping but attentive branches. At the slightest stirring of the wind the tree responded with a graceful dance. When the wind went quiet, so too the tree. Though surrounded by other trees (a spruce, a handsome birch, an elm), each with its unique character and distinctive beauty, the willow did not weep out of envy or jealousy. She had her own identity that none could deny. Though all the trees shared the same ground, thus providing a noteworthy unity, each tree displayed a distinct color and shape.

The willow teaches us receptivity and sensitivity. Watching it carefully is an exercise in discernment. The spiritual process of sorting out what is and what is not of God is no passive activity. Rather, through the gift of intuition one begins to develop a sense of congruence, a spiritual feeling for what fits and what is ajar. There is a way of seeing and sensing (indeed, of being) that transcends reason; there is an affinity caused by love that leads to authentic knowledge. The willow knows the breeze though it cannot be seen; the willow is rooted in the earth and towers to the sky; the willow accepts its gifts and limitations without jealousy. These dispositions underlie a courageous, discerning heart that seeks to do the truth in love.

We human willows need to learn the lessons of silence, waiting, trust, flexibility (the latest of the beatitudes), and courage. In silence we hear God's silent music. Through patience we adjust to God's timing. In confidence that the sun will shine and daily nourishment will be given, we embrace with joy our radical dependency. By giving up our categories and false idols we bend to the Spirit's will and experience the ecstasy of surrender. Through fortitude we withstand in grace the winter's harshness and less kind seasons. Willow-watching mirrors life. The Lord encourages us to learn a lesson from the fig tree; its cousin, the swaying willow, has its lessons as well.

Willow-watching challenges a disposition that dominates the contemporary scene: control. Training in management theory and organizational skills has nurtured the arts of efficiency and effectiveness, and happily so. But the transfer of theory and skills into the spiritual domain, unless done with proper adaptation, can be ruinous for the individual and the larger social whole. The danger lies in our attempt to manage God, to substitute our plans for his, to make God into our image and likeness. We in essence declare not just July 4th as a day of independence but every day as autonomous. We have become our own person!

Delicate balance is needed here. How to take initiative and yet be responsive? How to become receptive without falling into a quietism? How to work diligently and yet rely totally upon the grace of God? The willow, grounded in God and nourished in the divine milieu, must tend both to its own needs and yet provide sun-driven pilgrims with shade. Its balance and wisdom must be ours. A fine instructor, the weeping willow.

Belly-laughing: An Exercise in Expansiveness

"Laughter of any sort may be considered a religious exercise for it bears witness to the soul's emancipation."[2] G. K. Chesterton, in his classic work *Orthodoxy*, conjectures on divine laughter:

> I say with reverence; there was in that shattering personality [Jesus] a thread that must called shyness. There was something that He hid from all men when He went up a mountain to pray. There was something that He covered constantly by abrupt silence or impetuous isolation. There was some one thing that was too great for God to show when He walked upon our earth; and I have sometimes fancied it was His mirth.[3]

The role of humor in the spiritual life has been given inadequate attention. Yet we can be assured of one thing: laughter helps us deal with the burdens of life as few other things can. The oddity of truth, the eccentricities of the human spirit, the paradoxical nature of existence itself provide us, not only with enigma, but with exhilaration.

If a picture is worth a thousand words, a good belly-laugh is worth three psychiatric sessions (possibly four). Laughter, far distant from the nervous, superficial giggle, is expansive and therefore freeing. Our narrow lives are broken open, at least for the moment. Laughter, however short-lived, controls our body and spirit and enables us to experience the bittersweet of life. We come out of laughter into free air having gained a new perspective and having experienced a therapeutic catharsis. Laughter momentarily paralyzes our behavior thereby lightening our responsibility and simultaneously moving us out of the sometimes stagnant intellectual realm. Thrown into the affective, gut-level domain, we are stripped of control and are embraced by a small, strange deity, a deity we call Risibility.

Such emancipation cannot be purchased or planned; it is a gift to be tasted and treasured.

---

2. See William James, *The Varieties of Religious Experience* (New York: Modern Library, 1946), 76

3. G. K. Chesterton, *Orthodoxy* (New York: Doubleday & Co., 1959), 160.

Spirituality is serious business, some will argue. No room for flippancy here. Yes, spirituality is a serious and noble process, so much so that it retrains these qualities to the degree that perspective is nurtured and maintained. Laughter keeps the focus that allows one's spiritual growth to be integrated and human. Spirituality without laughter becomes heavy and rigid, deadly and abhorrent. It loses one of the universal characteristics identified with saintliness: joy! A spirituality that contracts the human spirit and that narrows life is to be shunned. Humorless spiritualities are marked by excessive introversion, a narrow fanaticism, a distorted theology. Perhaps a major cause for the rise of atheism in our time results from a concept of God that is static and narrow, devoid of life and empty of all humor. It is interesting to note a reflection from the Vatican II document *Gaudium et Spes:*

> Yet others have such a faulty notion of God that when they disown this product of the imagination their denial has no reference to the God of the Gospel.... Believers can thus have more than a little to do with the rise of atheism. To the extent that they are careless about their instruction in the faith, or present its teaching falsely, or even fail in their religious, moral, or social life, they must be said to conceal rather than to reveal the true nature of God and of religion. (no. 19)

Our conception of God is a major determinant of our spiritual lives. The living and true God, a God who demands righteousness but also a God of joy and laughter, of suffering and hope, is revealed through Jesus, who walked and laughed with his people.

Story-telling: An Exercise in Revelation

The power of story-telling lies in its ability to transform our fundamental attitudes and values. This transformation in turn affects our moral decisions and thereby alters our destiny. An interesting phenomenon occurs whenever a speaker leaves the land of abstraction and utters those magic words: "Once upon a time...." Heads are raised in expectations; hearts begin a happy fibrillation; a subtle energy enters the blood stream. Every story in which light shines in the darkness (a light that the darkness cannot overcome) is a sacred story and thus transformative.

Spirituality is essentially a story, a story about God and us. If we read God's autobiography well (and the chapters are Creation, Covenant, Redemption, Pentecost), love is revealed. If we appropriate the story and make it our own, then our lives become lives of gracious giving and receiving. Accidentals will change from age to age, from culture to culture, but the plot (ever thickening) remains the same. A light shines in the darkness, life conquers death, hope triumph over despair.

Spiritual health is abetted if we take time to develop our memory, that great and vast storehouse wherein we file away for future reference those stories that assist us in interpreting life. Meaning is necessary for full life; memory helps us to retain those significant moments of history that have shaped and molded the human heart. David's divine election and the tragedy of his adultery and murder; Jeremiah's turbulent call and struggle to accept God's will; Job's plight of suffering and temptations to despair: all stories of God touching human life; all stories of our own journey as we seek the face of God. Our memory banks are precious reservoirs that need our constant tending and concern.

Our culture, stressing immediacy and plagued with an explosion of knowledge, fails to reverence the memory. The sheer volume of facts overwhelms our finite capacity to recall what is truly significant. Thus our libraries, glutted with fat tomes, have become surrogate storehouses. What all this means is that the silos of the soul remain empty and when solitude does come, we rumble around a hallow echo chamber. A test question to evaluate this observation: if suddenly transported to a distant planet, what stories could we tell, what poems could we recite, what songs could we sing?

Spirituality, our call to a quality life in God, demands the cornerstone of a good memory. Without memory direction cannot be maintained; with memory hope becomes powerless; without memory darkness reigns. Forgetfulness has the horrendous consequence of isolating individuals and communities from the context of time and space. A sense of integration (wholeness) is conditioned on the retention of key components of life held in the treasury of the memory. Practice keeps us aware of these components; actions put them into a meaningful whole. The listening and telling of stories is an exercise of great spiritual significance.

Basket-weaving: An Exercise in Creativity

Madeleine L'Engle once commented: "Creativity opens us to revelation, and when our high creativity is lowered to two percent, so is our capacity to see angels, to walk on water, to talk with unicorns"[4] Whether it's basket-weaving, cookie-making, or simply planting flowers, we find a great treasure in our call to be creative. This powerful gift brings life to others as well as to ourselves. Our very identity, being part creator and part creature, is wrapped up in the mysterious process of life-giving that we call creativity.

Creativity is limited only by an undeveloped imagination. One of the challenges is to activate our ossified imagination so that our creative energies can be channeled in exciting and nourishing ways. The classics of Western spirituality are filled with images that help people understand their relationship with God: Catherine of Siena uses the image of a bridge to show the role of Christ in redemption; John of the Cross takes the image of fire and the log to symbolize the process of purgation and growth in the Lord; Teresa uses the symbol of a castle to depict the stages of spiritual development. Imagination, stimulated through analogy, deepens our knowledge of God's grace and concern.

A constant danger in spirituality is a sterile and blind conformity. Having but a single pattern of prayer, reaching out to but

---

4. Madeleine L'Engle, *Walking on Water: Reflections on Faith and Art* (Wheaton, Ill.: Harold Shaw Publishers, 1980), 75.

one need among so many, attending to a single theology can be confining, nay devastating. The causes of such unhealthy conformity are many: fear of change, overwhelming need for security, overconcern about the opinion of others, compulsive patterns, buying into being outer-directed. While not denying the necessity and beauty of a healthy conformity (one that finds us in line with what is true and good), there is a constant drifting into patterns of routine that block the creative dimension of life and that mutilate our imagination. Excitement and enthusiasm are thereby lost and life can become sour.

The faculty of imagination needs exercise if our creative genius is to develop. Here our spiritual lives can be greatly enriched by a love for and study of the sciences and arts. The achievements in these fields, imaginatively designed and skillfully implemented, teach us many lessons about the grandeur of God. Once again we might well learn to play the masterpieces of music, dwell with loving attention on the creations of great artists, stand in awe of the discoveries and inventions of science. In so doing, our own imagination might be activated and used to share the life that has been given to us.

Conclusion: An Exercise in Wisdom

Knowing when to stop is no small feat in the spiritual realm. This is specially true for an eclectic. So much more could be said, so many more books could be read, so many more roads might be taken. I would like, however to defend eclecticism against its critics, though noted purists. Though lacking unity, eclecticism benefits humankind by tapping a variety of sources without limiting itself to a single system of thought or practice. Though seeming rather scattered, eclecticism gathers the pieces that one day must be integrated; a single philosophy/theology lacks wholeness because it never incorporates insight beyond its own perspective. Though messy and at times ambiguous, eclecticism is real and is willing to be patient on its road to clarity. An eclectic spirituality admittedly has drawbacks, but fewer than its benefits.

Leading a nomadic life simply means that we are a pilgrim

people. Although we many be somewhat stationary as far as geography would have it, the spiritual life means that we must be willing to move all the way from Ur to Haran, like our father Abraham. Whenever God calls, we must be ready and willing to respond with generosity and whole-heartedness. A nomadic life is a call to grow, not to stand still. This calls for an openness of spirit, a flexibility of will, a trust in a promise. Not to grow verges on the edge of the ultimate sin. Stagnation has few rivals to first place in the hall of sin's infamy.

Growth in the spiritual life might well be aided by stargazing, willow-watching, belly-laughing, story-telling, basket-weaving. These are only a few of the exercises for eclectic nomads. Others on the list: toe-tapping — an exercise in joy; kite-flying — an exercise in courage; river-running — an exercise in giving up control; angleworm-assisting — an exercise in compassion; tree-climbing — an exercise in perspective. And the list goes on and on and on.

Chapter 7

GAUDEAMUS IGITUR: IN DEFENSE OF JOY

Though St. Paul never sang the once popular "Gaudeamus Igi-tur" ("therefore let us rejoice") we know from his letter to the Philippians that a song of joy filled his very being. In fact, the vocation to joy stands firmly at the center of a Christian life. But Paul does not simply express this calling; he provides bountiful evidence, a number of "igiturs," to support his conviction that joyfulness should characterize the following of Christ Jesus. This essay extracts five reasons underlying Paul's conviction that rejoicing in the Lord is a basic baptismal call.

The twentieth century finds the vocation to joy unwar-ranted. The modern skeptic can quickly document reasons for sadness, despondency, and despair. Rampant crime, violence on the street and in the home, world wars, the suffering of the innocent, broken relationships, harsh discrimination, ha-tred and apathy — these are simply the beginning of a long litany of painful facts. Hearing this our spirits sag, hope seems useless, we become suspicious of existence itself. Need we be surprised with the observation that Christianity is often joyless!

We must not deny reality. The council fathers of Vatican II demanded that the community of believers in Jesus, the church, embrace the fullness of human life:

> The joys and hopes, the griefs and the anxieties of the men of this age, especially those who are poor or in any

way afflicted, these too are the joys and hopes, the griefs and anxieties of the followers of Christ. Indeed, nothing genuinely human fails to raise an echo in their hearts. For theirs is a community composed of men. United in Christ, they are led by the Holy Spirit in their journey to the kingdom of their Father and they have welcomed the news of salvation which is meant for every man. That is why this community realizes that it is truly and intimately linked with mankind and its history. ("The Church in the Modern World," no. 1)

The Latin title for this document is "Gaudium et Spes" — joy and hope. In the face of the muddiness of human life, in spite of its sufferings and anxieties, despite our individual and collective sin, we are called to have hope and joy. St. Paul's correspondence with the people of Philippi sets forth a case in defense of this deep and challenging vocation to joy.

Presence

Joy is experienced when someone we love or someone who loves us is near. If we were to examine the happiest moments of our personal lives, I would conjecture that for most of us those experiences happened when we were surrounded by people we care for in a radical way. The circumstances (be they a play, dinner, a walk on the beach) are strictly secondary; the primary fact is that the one we love is near and the overflow of this is joy. Paul writes to his people: "Rejoice in the Lord always! I say it again. Rejoice! Everyone should see how unselfish you are. The Lord is near" (Phil. 4:4–5). In faith Paul realized that the Lord was with him and with the people. He would share with another community the profound mystery of the indwelling Christ: "the life I live now is not my own; Christ is living in me" (Gal. 2:20). Such intimacy is a great cause for joy. Yet this is in no way romantic. There is no denial that life is often difficult and filled with pain. St. Paul could match anyone in a show of scars. But despite his frequent physical and psychological distress, a deep and lasting joy filled his spirit. The Lord's nearness explains a portion of that mystery.

Abbot Marmion once wrote: "Joy is the knowledge that I possess something that is good." Substituting "someone" for something we might come slightly closer to the heart of the matter. The disciples in the upper room, fearful and ashamed, suddenly shed their discouragement when they experienced the presence of the risen Lord. With the gift of his peace, i.e., the gift of himself, they rejoiced. The human pilgrimage is filled with the knowledge that we indeed possess someone who is good: the experience of receiving a love letter, the meaningful visitation in an illness, the invitation to become a friend, the touch of a human hand on a lonely day. Joy comes with that affective knowledge that our need, the basic psychological atom, has been wondrously filled.

Another source in Scripture besides St. Paul that confirms that the presence of the beloved results in joy is found in Psalm 16. Here we pray: "You will show me the path to life, fullness of joys in your presence, the delights at your right hand forever" (16:11). A reverse image might help to clarify this. Air-conditioned unhappiness tells of the situation in which we have the finest things that comfort the body but inside there is a gnawing emptiness and discontent. In other words, joy cannot be sustained simply by possessions, though our culture would have us believe this to be true. A faith of any depth reveals that being in relationship is at the heart of happiness and of joy. Joy in its fullness is not a solitary experience. Thus C. S. Lewis writes in one of his novels: "We have known great joys together."[1]

Truth

Joy is consequent upon truth. Two passages in the letter to the Philippians focus on this point:

> I give thanks to my God every time I think of you — which is constantly in every prayer I utter — rejoicing, as I plead

---

1. C. S. Lewis, *The Last Battle* (New York: Collier Books, 1956), 99.

on your behalf, at the way you have all continually helped promote the gospel from the very first day. (1:3–5)

... Christ is being proclaimed! That is what brings me joy. (1:18)

The truth is Christ Jesus. Joy comes when the truth of his person and his message (the gospel) is proclaimed and internalized. When this happens we are set free from darkness and slavery. Paul's own conversion underlies these reflections. He experienced the person of Christ Jesus and throughout his apostolic journey continued to encounter the redeeming truth of God's love. Being in touch with this truth, joy pulsated through his very being.

Augustine, in his magnificent autobiography, states that "the mind feeds on that in which it finds joy." Our lives are nourished and joyful as we grow in the knowledge of our God, a God of love. Further, the people whom God sends into our lives are revelations of God's truth. We ponder our friendships and see therein the mystery of truth and concern. Though at times the divine and human encounters of our lives are painful because honest, we can be assured that when the truth is spoken and then lived, joy will soon follow.

We can draw an important and highly pragmatic conclusion from all this: joy in the modern world will be conditioned by the quality of evangelization. Evangelization is a complex process in which the kingdom of God is proclaimed and Jesus is preached as Lord of all. When this mission is done well the possibility of joy is high. The news proclaimed is truly good; the freedom to be won is indeed liberating; the life of grace freely offered is vibrant and radiant. It may well be that a lack of joy today stems from inadequate evangelizers. Improper and oppressive techniques, misguided and insensitive language, lack of zeal and example, inner resistance: these are all obstacles to the effective sharing of God's word and God's love. Today the church urgently needs competent and loving disciples who live the word in hope and proclaim it with joy.

Unity

Oneness between and among people promotes joy. Paul's urgent plea speaks to all ages:

> In the name of the encouragement you owe me in Christ, in the name of the solace that love can give, of fellowship in spirit, compassion and pity, I beg you: make my joy complete by your unanimity, possessing the one love, united in spirit and ideals. (Phil. 2:1–2)

In this vision there are three ingredients essential for the unity of any gathering of people: consciousness of identity, agreement about certain values, a common spirit. The source of identity and oneness is life in Christ, a common fellowship flowing from the faith fact of being sons and daughters of a common Father. Further, the Spirit of Christ and the Father has been given to them. Awareness of who they are makes community a possibility. Second, love is the central value about which they agree. A life based on radical concern and unselfishness in imitation of Christ is the Christian call. Third, the environment created in unity is permeated by a spirit of compassion and pity. This makes possible the art and practice of forgiveness, thus sacramentalizing the redemptive work of Jesus. The cross and resurrection take on meaning in such a lifestyle. Paul's joy is only half realized until unanimity in all three areas is achieved. Thus joy is essentially communal. Only when others share fully in the experience of love and the Christian ideal can Paul be completely happy.

Underlying this search for oneness that promotes joy is the Father's will. Jesus was consumed by the vision that "all may be one." Keenly aware of division and alienation that tragically separated people from people and humankind from the Father, Jesus' central mission was one of reconciliation. Paul knew his mystery from the inside, knowing himself to be divided within and without. Thus, he, like Jesus, strove for the coming of the reign of God in every human heart. Meister Eckhart captured well the relationship between God's will and joy:

> Perfectly to will what God wills, to want what he wants, is to have joy; but if one's will is not quite in unison with God's, there is no joy. May God help us to be in tune with him![2]

The unity/joy theme is a constant biblical call. John the Evangelist reiterates Paul's experience of incompleteness of joy unless shared:

> What we have seen and heard we proclaim in turn to you so that you may share life with us. This fellowship of ours is with the Father and with his Son, Jesus Christ. Indeed, our purpose in writing you this is that our joy may be complete. (1 John 1:3–4)

Rugged individualism is incompatible with the gospel message. Christianity is communal and the constant refrain that joy is incomplete when experienced alone drives the community aspect home. Our joy and peace will always be diminished if others do not share in it. Fullness of joy comes only when all share the unifying good of a common life. Practically, this theology of joy has powerful ramifications: guilt when our wealth is not shared, unrest when basic human rights are denied, anxiety when dehumanizing attitudes and practices find a home within our lives. Whatever causes division and alienation must be the object of our concern and action. Thus, joy desired for all will lead us into active involvement in social reform. Joy is a first cousin to justice and peace.

Meaningfulness

Joy provides the energy and vision to lead a meaningful life. Without this precious gift and grace, futility can begin to control life and lead to depression and angst. Life, if there is to be any joy at all, must have meaning; action must be purposeful. Paul experienced joy in his ministry because the mission upon which he was sent was rich in meaning to him. He

---

2. *Meister Eckhart,* trans. Raymond B. Blakney (New York: Harper Torchbooks, 1941), 42.

was an ambassador of Christ, an agent of reconciliation. He writes:

> As I look to the Day of Christ, you give me cause to boast that I did not run the race in vain or work to no purpose. Even if my life is to be poured out as a libation over the sacrificial service of your faith, I am glad of it and rejoice with all of you. May you be glad on the same score, and rejoice with me! (Phil. 2:17–18)

Joy here has a certain contingency. Because the people responded in faith to the gospel proclamation, Paul knew that the race undertaken and the work so ardently performed were not futile. The response of people who opened their lives to Christ caused joy in Paul's heart. Not all of Paul's preaching met with such success. The heaviness of his heart can be easily discerned as the preached word fell on deaf ears or when the message once received was abandoned. Paul is candid; his emotions are close to the surface. We know when joy filled his heart; we also know the discouragement that shattered the ever-fragile grace of joy. Meaningfulness deals with how we interpret the experiences of life. For some, life is sheer toil and pain, lacking purpose or design. All ends in death and it makes little difference how one spends the short life span allotted. Others, in faith, find that every moment is a matter of grace. God is always working and it is the task of life to discern God's presence and respond to God's call and touch. Many perhaps fall some place in between, finding meaning in certain situations and despair in others. Interpretation of life is no abstract matter; it colors every moment of every day. Catherine of Siena offers a vision that was part of her own experience:

> To everything they find joy and the fragrance of the rose. This is true not only of good things; even when they see something that is clearly sinful they do not pass judgment, but rather feel a holy and genuine compassion, praying for the sinner and saying with perfect humility, "Today it

is your turn: tomorrow it will be mine unless divine grace
holds me up."[3]

Meaningfulness escapes us, as does joy, as long as we have not
dealt with the large questions of identity and destiny. Unless
an individual or a community has a sense of who they are and
where they are going, no action or lifestyle has ultimate significance. Joy is grounded for the faith person in an affective
knowledge that reveals that one is loved and called into being
by God, that one is destined to dwell in God's presence for eternity, that being a loving, compassionate person is at the heart
of existence. In this broad context the joy of life comes from
making choices that bring us and others into the fullness of
our destiny (oneness with God) and that allow decisions to express who we really are. Joy resides in a vast arena and is rooted
deeply in life. Paul entered that arena in search of this grace and
found it; he plunged into the depths of life and touched the
mystery of a joyous God. In Christ, the Lord of joy, he found
meaning.

Love

Where authentic love is experienced, joy will always be found.
Paul's delight is obvious: "It gave me great joy in the Lord that
your concern for me bore fruit once more" (Phil. 4:10). That
wonderful leap from thinking about to doing indicates that love
is truly genuine. Paul planted many seeds in proclaiming the
mystery of Jesus and sharing the command of love. Now the
harvest is seen: people bearing fruit in their radical concern
and respect for others. Harvest time is joyous: all the labor has
not been in vain, the produce will nourish body and spirit, a
goal has been attained. And with the celebration there is joy.

In Nikos Kazantzakis's *Zorba the Greek* the statement is
made: "My joys here are great, because they are very simple
and spring from the everlasting elements: the pure air, the sun,

---

3. *Catherine of Siena: The Dialogue*, trans. and introduction by Suzanne
Noffke, O.P. (New York: Paulist Press, 1980), 190.

the sea and the wheaten loaf."[4] The gifts of love are often very simple: the unexpected flower, the gracious nod of recognition, the gentle word of affirmation, a happy memory recalled. Though the love may seem simple the joy is profound. It is in the everlasting elements of life that joy and love abide: friendships, conversations, silent walks, union of mind and body, the cup of cold water. Love and joy are common elements composing the basic nucleus of life.

Though love and joy, the fruit born of genuine spirituality, might be labeled as sheer grace, this grace is the result of a decision. God decided to love us and this love has become visible in Christ Jesus. Thus joy is premised on a decision. Now we too can make that same decision to incarnate God's love through our personal histories. In making this choice, joy comes into existence. This need not happen. We can decide not to love; we can withhold our affirmation of others; we need not get involved in meeting needs. Sadness and woe are then born. What tremendous power individuals carry within their hearts. The quantity and quality of joy is often dependent upon our exercise of freedom. Jesus, in calling us to be the salt and light of the world, is calling us to bring his joy into being. To fail in this mission is the most grievous tragedy of all.

Conclusion

"Gaudeamus igitur" — therefore let us rejoice! Why? Five Pauline igiturs: The Lord is near (presence); Jesus (truth) is proclaimed; community is for real (unity); life is significant (meaningful); people are concerned (love). There are reasons for joy, and whenever we are loving, offering meaning, sharing truth, creating oneness, truly being present, we continue to foster the joy of Christ in our time. One last witness might speak in our defense of joy, Mother Teresa of Calcutta:

Joy is prayer; joy is strength; joy is love; joy is a net of love by which you can catch souls. God loves a cheerful

---

4. Nikos Kazantzakis, *Zorba the Greek* (New York: Simon and Schuster, Ballantine Books, 1952), 104

giver. She gives most who gives with joy. The best way to show our gratitude to God and the people is to accept everything with joy. A joyful heart is the inevitable result of a heart burning with love. Never let anything so fill you with sorrow as to make you forget the joy of the Christ risen.[5]

---

5. *A Gift for God: Mother Teresa of Calcutta* (New York: Harper & Row, 1980), 77.

Chapter 8

QUAKER SPIRITUALITY: CONCEPTS AND CONCERNS

Dialogue promotes appreciation and understanding when undertaken with sincerity and knowledge. By entering into serious reflection with another human being or a rich tradition, we open ourselves to new insights and often to a different worldview. At times we will agree with and assimilate much of the conversation; at other times, we will question, perhaps reject certain tenets and propositions. Civility demands that our dialogues be characterized by candidness, respect, honesty, and openness. No one person or tradition has a corner on the whole truth. We have much to learn from each other. Indeed, authentic dialogue is a precious phenomenon, too seldom experienced because of arrogance, prejudice, and sheer indifference.

The Quaker tradition has much to offer to the ongoing conversion of life and religious faith. The vision and values of the Quakers have had a major influence both within and outside their community. In a recent edition of Quaker thought, *Quaker Spirituality: Selected Writings,* we are given a resource manual containing selected passages from the journals of George Fox and John Woolman as well as some of the theological reflections of Caroline Stephen, Rufus Jones, and

Thomas Kelley.[1] Experiences are presented first, then the more philosophical and theological observations. Although both the journals and theological reflections are selective in nature, they provide a representative picture of the main line of Quaker thought.

This essay presents several key concepts that seem to be central to Quaker spirituality. Direct quotations are followed by a personal commentary. The reader is encouraged to go to the primary sources for the full context of the ideas presented. My personal conviction is that we have much to learn from our Quaker brothers and sisters. Their deep faith life and their concern for social issues demonstrate an integrated spirituality. While being very much God-centered, they do not neglect matters of global responsibility nor refuse to do the work of justice.

Silence

> It seems to me that nothing but silence can heal the wounds made by disputations in the region of the unseen. No external help, at any rate, has ever in my own experience proved so penetratingly efficacious as the habit of joining in a public worship based upon silence. Its primary attraction for me was in the fact that it pledged me to nothing, and left me altogether undisturbed to seek for help in my own way. But before long I began to be aware that the united and prolonged silences had a far more direct and powerful effect than this. They soon began to exercise a strangely subduing and softening effect upon my mind. There used, after a while, to come upon me a deep sense of awe, as we sat together and waited — for what? In my heart of hearts I knew in whose name we were met together, and who was truly in the midst of us. Never before had his influence re-

---

1. *Quaker Spirituality: Selected Writings,* edited and introduced by Douglas V. Steere (New York: Paulist Press, 1984); all quotations are taken from the text with the author and page indicated.

vealed itself to me with so much power as in those quiet assemblies.[2]

~

These silences, during which all children of our family were hushed with a kind of awe, were very important features of my spiritual development.[3]

~

Very often in these meetings for worship, which held usually for two hours, there were long periods of silence, for we never had singing to fill the gaps. I do not think anybody ever told me what the silence was for. It does not seem necessary to explain Quaker silence to children. They *feel* what it means. They do not know how to use very long periods of hush, but there is something in short, living, throbbing times of silence which *finds* the child's submerged life and stirs it to nobler living and holier aspiration. I doubt if there is any method of worship which works with a subtler power or which brings into operation in the interior life a more effective moral and spiritual culture.[4]

~

The silence we value is not the mere outward silence of the lips. It is a deep quietness of heart and mind, a laying aside of all preoccupations with passing things — yes, even with the workings of our own minds; a resolute fixing of the heart upon that which is unchangeable and eternal. This "silence of the flesh" appears to us to be the essential preparation for any act of true worship. It is also, we believe, the essential condition at all times of inward illumination.[5]

Silence is a rare commodity in this last segment of the twentieth century. Noise, often of great intensity, bombards

2. Stephen, 249.
3. Jones, 263.
4. Jones, 268.
5. Stephen, 250.

us on every side from the shrieking police siren to the boom box carried along city streets, from the blare of the TV to the incessant chatter of friend and acquaintance. Even the early dawn and late night hours are frequented by the distractions of the human voice and our ubiquitous technology. When exaggerated or too frequent, noise turns into a form of violence, breaking down our sensitivities and sensibilities. The divine whisper is no longer heard and in this lies the greatest of tragedies.

Silence is much more than the absence of sound. It is a way of being, a reverent stance before creation. Silence is that quiet receptivity which allows us to encounter "Reality." Silence is a physical stillness but even more a spiritual hush that makes our hearts hospitable to God's coming. Silence is an emptiness so deep, a sense of being so un-preoccupied that marvelous things happen within the soul. As E. Herman writes in her *Creative Prayer:* "If we read the biographies of the great and wise, be they statesmen or priests, teachers or poets, Roman Catholics or Quakers, we shall find that they were men of long silences and deep ponderings."[6]

The experience of silence is not to be romanticized. Some silences are deadly and destructive. We need to be schooled in the art of constructive silences. Our educational theories and our liturgical celebrations must reclaim the power of silence and its influence on the shaping of the human spirit. Again E. Herman is helpful: "We have yet to accept and act upon the axiom that the cultivation of a habit of silence is an integral part of all true education; and that children, so far from looking upon a demand for silence as an unnatural and intolerable imposition, have an inborn aptitude for quietness."[7] Why is there in our day such an uneasiness when things become quiet? Perhaps such experiences put us at the disposal of some higher power, whereas constant talk provides at least

---

6. E. Herman, *Creative Prayer* (Cincinnati: Forward Movement Publications, n.d.), 31.

7. Ibid., 33

the appearance that we are in control. The Quakers' traditional respect for silence helps them to foster union with God.

Experience

> We have here, then, a type of Christianity which begins with experience rather than with dogma.... As the Reformation proceeded, the old dogma of the Church assumed an ever-increasing importance and in the end doctrine was raised to a status which overpassed anything known in the medieval Church.[8]

> ~

> Nothing, I believe, can really teach us the nature and meaning of inspiration but personal experience of it. That we may all have such experience if we will but attend to the divine influences in our own hearts, is the cardinal doctrine of Quakerism.[9]

> ~

> We were taught by renewed experience to labour for an inward stillness, at no time to seek for words, but to live in the spirit of Truth and utter that to the people which Truth opened in us.[10]

Experience means presence and encounter. Whether personal or vicarious, active or passive, positive or negative, experience puts us in contact with reality. Some experiences that are painful and confrontative elicit a movement to construct defensive mechanisms (e.g., rationalizations, projections, illusions) in order to avoid suffering. In yielding to such movements we may indeed survive, but at the cost of personal integrity. The challenge is to be open to everyday experience through which God enters our life. Openness to the moment makes possible authentic experience. Two major factors condition the quality of our experience: disposition and processing. By means of the first we cultivate the soil of our minds and hearts to what

---

8. Jones, 277.
9. Stephen, 247.
10. Woolman, 172.

is happening in our lives. By means of processing, we assimilate (appropriate, internalize) our experiences in an integrative fashion.

At times, experience competes with dogma. Ideally these need not be in opposition. Dogma (a belief system articulating in propositions and specific statements what we hold to be true) is of great importance in every tradition. Yet dogma is once-removed from experience. To make a statement about my belief in God is far different from dwelling in God's presence. Dogmas provide a meaning structure through words and language; experience provides a complex encounter filled with feelings, questions, imperatives. Dogmas give us a sense of control whereas experiences cannot be managed all that well. Finally, dogmas are expressed predominantly in cognitive terms, whereas experiences find expression in affective language.

God breaks into history in many ways as seen in the revelation contained in Scripture and the traditions reflecting the histories of faith communities. These avenues are not to be treated lightly. Quaker spirituality gives emphasis to the interior experience of God's touch and word. Their emphasis is, as it were, not in the reference manuals telling "about" God, but in the primary source of God's immediate presence to the individual and to the community. Those who sit in stillness and wait with patience will not be disappointed. Experience is given the spotlight (centrality) for the Quakers; other traditions within Christianity will highlight dogma, Scripture, or tradition itself. Balance is needed since God uses various channels as He wills.

Integration of Prayer and Action

The straightest road to social gospel runs through the profound mystical experience. The paradox of true mysticism is that individual experience leads to social passion, that the nonuseful engenders the greatest utility.[11]

~

---

11. Kelley, 306.

I saw, as I had not seen before, that the religion of these men [Friends] was not merely an affair of the meeting house; not merely a way to get to heaven. It was something which made them thoughtful of others and ready to sacrifice for others. I saw how it worked itself out in practical deeds of kindness and righteousness.[12]

~

I kept to meetings, spent First-days after noon chiefly in reading the Scriptures and other good books, and was early convinced in mind that true religion consisted in an inward life, wherein the heart doth love and reverence God the Creator and learn to exercise true justice and goodness, not only towards all men but also towards the brute creatures; that as the mind was moved on an inward principle to love God as an invisible, incomprehensible being, on the same principle it was moved to love him in all his manifestations in the visible world; that as by his breath the flame of life was kindled in all animal and sensitive creatures, to say we love God as unseen and at the same time exercise cruelty towards the least creature moving in his life, or by life derived from him, was a contradiction in itself.[13]

In 1962 William Lynch, a Jesuit writer of rich imagination and insight, published *The Integrating Mind*, in which he stated that the human tendency to dichotomize, i.e., to make things either/or, is fatal to our understanding of reality. Either prayer or action, either reason or passion, either politics or religion! The challenge is to integrate the apparent opposites or seeming contradictions. Health, within the individual and society, depends upon the development of this wholistic approach to life.

A stereotype of Quaker spirituality depicts a group of people sitting in assembly completely absorbed in the inner life of

---

12. Jones, 272.
13. Woolman, 165.

silence and waiting. Unconcerned about social or political issues, they attempt to find their own peace regardless of what happens to the rest of the world. Such a caricature is rejected in fact and in theory. Indeed, Quaker spirituality holds that the inner life is central. The search for God and the power of silent prayer is the base from which all else flows. Yet what happens interiorly must find expression in concern for others and the world. The quotations above make this abundantly clear. The lived examples of the leaders within the Quaker tradition demonstrate social involvement and a hunger for justice which often involved great sacrifice and even imprisonment.

An integrated spirituality assumes that there is a rich interdependence among the essential elements of the faith life. What happens in the depth of one's interior life (prayer) provides vision and energy for outward action. The outer activities (service) become a reflection of God's word calling us to discipleship. Not to be excluded from this cartography of the spiritual life are acts of sacrifice (mortification, asceticism), times of extended withdrawal (retreats), periods of formal study (formation), experiences of radical change (ongoing conversion). The fabric is singular but it involves the interweaving of many threads. Even our personal (private?) spirituality is communal in that it impacts on the lives of others. Quaker spirituality is concerned with the diverse elements of the spiritual journey and attempts to bring them together in a unified whole.

Divine Center

Life is meant to be lived from the Center, a divine Center. Each of us can live such a life of amazing power and peace and serenity, of integration and confidence and simplified multiplicity, on one condition — that is, *if we really want to*. There is a divine Abyss within us all, a holy Infinite Center, a Heart, a Life who speaks in us and through us to the world. We have all heard this holy Whisper at times. At times we have followed the Whisper, and amazing equilibrium of life, amazing effectiveness of living set in. But too many of us have heeded the Voice only at times. Only at times have we submitted to his holy guidance. We have not counted this Holy Thing within us to be the most precious thing in the world. We have not surrendered *all else*, to attend to it alone. Let me repeat. Most of us, I fear have not surrendered all else, in order to attend to the Holy Within.[14]

~

There *is* a last Rock for your souls, a resting place of absolute peace and joy and power and radiance and security. There is a Divine Center into which your life can slip, a new and absolute orientation to God, a Center where you live with him, and out from which you see all life, through new and radiant vision, tinged with new sorrows and pangs, new joys unspeakable and full of glory.[15]

~

To that of God in you both I speak, and do beseech you both for the Lord's sake to return within, and wait to hear the voice of the Lord there; and waiting there, and keeping close to the Lord, a discerning will grow, that you may distinguish the voice of the stranger when ye hear it.[16]

St. Teresa of Avila, in her classic *The Interior Castle*, describes the interior life as a series of mansions or rooms within a castle, a metaphor for the soul. In the center dwells the Lord. Teresa delineates the obstacles blocking access to that innermost mansion. She also lists the various means by which that divine home can be reached. Her writings of the sixteenth century parallel some of the themes in Quaker spirituality. The "divine center" is one of them.

The question of where we live is not ultimately a question of physical geography. The roads we travel, the cities we live in, the nation in which we work and play are but one dimension of

---

14. Kelley, 304.
15. Kelley, 315.
16. Fox, 129.

space. Another aspect is our spiritual orientation: our perspective of reality, our basic values and attitudes, our conscience and disposition. It is here that we are challenged to attend to the voice of God; here is the essence of the spiritual life. It comes down to a matter of presence: either we become aware of God's presence, which is both immanent and transcendent, or we live outside our home in a meaningless universe. At some point a choice has to be made about our dwelling and our companionship. An act of surrender to a new axis — to a new center — is at the heart of conversion and transformation. A "no" here puts us east of Eden once again. We have lost our home and wander in exile.

Quaker spirituality emphasizes immanence. Although appreciating the relationship between the inner life and external activity, it does not emphasize the notion of God as surrounding and embracing all of creation as much as it stresses God's interior presence. Transcendence, although not denied, is simply not the object of extended reflection. Each tradition, given historical factors, makes such choices. Regardless, the inward journey demands deep faith and much courage. A call to return home must constantly be made, especially in a noisy world.

Concern

Against this cosmic suffering and cosmic responsibility we must set the special responsibility experienced in a *concern*. For a Quaker concern particularizes this cosmic tenderness. It brings to a definite and effective focus in some concrete task all that experience of love and responsibility which might evaporate, in its broad generality, into vague yearnings for a golden Paradise.[17]

~

The social concern of Friends is grounded in an experience — an experience of the love of God and of the impulse to saviourhood inherent in the fresh quickening of that life. Social concern is the dynamic Life of God

---

17. Kelley, 302.

at work in the world, made special and empathic and unique, particularized in each individual or group who is sensitive and tender in the leading-strings of love. A concern is God-initiated, often surprising, always holy, for the Life of God is breaking through into the world. Its execution is a peace and power and astounding faith and joy, for in unhurried serenity the Eternal is at work in the midst of time, triumphantly bringing all things up unto himself.[18]

~

I felt a certain awe because they always came with "a concern," which means that they had left their homes and had undertaken the long journey because they had received an unmistakable and irresistible call to go out and preach what was given them.[19]

The mystery of evil has perplexed the mind and heart of people throughout history. One description of evil involves the tendency to make abstract that which is concrete. For example, to bomb "a city" (somewhat of an abstraction) appears quite different from bombing a child, this specific group of people, this home for the elderly. By abstracting people into a nebulous "city" all kinds of things are justified. Goodness demands that we have "concerns," concerns for particular deeds and specific people. Broad generalities seldom motivate; specific concerns do.

The expression "nail things down" helps to identify a strong Quaker desire. Given the many social and global obligations placed on the shoulders of humankind, it becomes necessary to focus on specifics if we are to ameliorate the world. A key word is "particularize" — to make something specific, concrete, particular. To do this effectively, we must momentarily block out everything else. Thus philosophers are often paralyzed because of an inability to get away from the "big picture," from the tendency to see so many sides of so many issues. The opposite

---

18. Kelley, 303.
19. Jones, 268.

danger is to become a fanatic by being so absorbed in a special issue as to lose sight of its relationship to other values and aspects of reality. Meaning is then lost, as is sanity.

Quaker spirituality is a concerned spirituality. God's call is constant. The challenge is to make God's concerns our own. As Jim Wallis writes: "The people of God are known in the world for the same things for which God is known. God's people should care about the same things that God cares for. Our purposes and priorities are the same. We love the same things, hate the same things, take joy in the same things, and hurt over the same things that God does."[20] God takes the initiative in moving us to action. Discernment and courage are essential at this juncture. Discernment helps us to sort out the many voices that seek to attract our attention. This gift also helps us to know specifically what it is that God is calling us to do. Courage empowers us to carry that discernment into action. It does little good to hear but not to live the call. In fact, it causes a spiritual disease which is truly cancerous. Proof of discipleship is to live these "concerns" — indeed, "don't talk of love, show me!"

Tenderness

And now, as I had experienced the love of God through Jesus Christ to redeem me from many pollutions and to be a succor to me through a sea of conflicts, with which no person was fully acquainted, and as my heart was often enlarged in this heavenly principle, I felt a tender compassion for the youth who remained entangled in snares like those which had entangled me. From one month to another this love and tenderness increased, and my mind was more strongly engaged for the good of my fellow creatures.[21]

~

My exercise was heavy and I was deeply bowed in spirit before the Lord, who was pleased to favour with the sea-

---

20. James Wallis, *The Call to Conversion* (San Francisco: Harper & Row, 1981), 143.
21. Woolman, 167.

soning of Truth which wrought a tenderness amongst us, and the subject was mutually handled in a calm and peaceable spirit. And at length feeling my mind released from that burden which I had been under, I took my leave of them in a good degree of satisfaction, and by the tenderness they manifested in regard to the practice and the concern several of them expressed in relations.[22]

~

And after sitting a short time, I stood up and in some tenderness of spirit acquainted them with the nature of my visit and that a concern for their good had made me willing to come thus far to see them — all in a few short sentences, which some of them, understanding, interpreted to the others; and there appeared gladness amongst them.[23]

In his letter to the Galatians, St. Paul speaks about tenderness or gentleness as one sign of God's presence. Individuals and communities can measure the reality of their inner transformation by means of the qualities of love, joy, peace, patience, kindness, goodness, trustworthiness, gentleness and self-control. The quality of tenderness speaks more of tonality than of a particular deed or word. The tender person has a certain style or manner of reverence revealing the texture of the heart. L. Boros speaks of tenderness in these terms: "Tenderness is nothing weak or inferior. It is the height of feeling which protects the lovely things of the world, encounters them with respect and treats them with the dignity of restraint."[24]

Tenderness is a consequence of grace. It is gift. Although an individual cooperates in being tender, essentially tenderness is the working of God's life in the deepest recesses of the heart. Authentic tenderness is devoid of romantic sentimentalism, as is every true movement of grace. Rooted in reality, the

---

22. Woolman, 197.
23. Woolman, 211.
24. Ladislaus Boros, *Hidden God,* trans. Erika Young (New York: Seabury Press, 1971), 89.

tender person knows the fragileness of all life. With a sense of vulnerability, the graced person protects and promotes the beauties of creation. There is something eternal about the grace of tenderness. Emily Dickinson gives it poetic expression: "Yet Tenderness has not a Date — it comes — and overwhelms. The time before it was — was naught, so why establish it? And all the time to come it is, which abrogates the time."[25]

In its strong opposition to violence, Quaker spirituality is automatically drawn into the virtue of tenderness. The stranglehold is replaced by the gentle embrace; the sharp word by words that overflow with concern; the hurried deed by a quiet rhythm of life that gives evidence that God's providence is at work and that we are not in full control. All of us will frequently fail in this regard, but the ideal is important. We must stand open to receive that gentleness which alone fosters peace.

Conclusion

Pope Paul VI, in his classic encyclical *Ecclesiam Suam*, writes brilliantly about dialogue. Unity will happen only when we communicate at a deep level. The ecumenical movement challenges us to become increasingly aware of other traditions and their experience of God. The documents of Vatican Council II frequently stress the need to talk to and with our brothers and sisters of different beliefs and ideologies. This brief essay is but a beginning to the process. I would encourage the reader to read *Quaker Spirituality: Selected Writings*. The introduction by Douglas V. Steere provides an excellent background for Quakerism. Further, Steere's own works — *Where Words Come From, On Being Present Where You Are, On Speaking Out of the Silence* — are references that expand on the Paulist Press work.

Quaker spirituality strives for that unity with God and unity among people that permeate all true spiritual journeys. Their

---

25. See Richard B. Sewall, *The Life of Emily Dickinson* (New York: Farrar, Straus and Giroux, 1974), 659.

strengths and weaknesses must be carefully noted. Their examples of success and failure must be respected. I am grateful for their contributions to history and to my own personal journey.